Holy Dirt, Sacred Earth

A Dowser's Journey in New Mexico

Robert Egby

Author of the Award Winning

The Quest of the Radical Spiritualist

INSIGHTS: The Healing Paths of the Radical Spiritualist

Three Mile Point Publishing
Chaumont, NY

Copyright © 2012 Robert Egby

Published by:
Three Mile Point Publishing
26941 Three Mile Point Road
Chaumont, NY 13622
www.threemilepointpublishing.com
Phone: 315-654-2060

Book formatting and cover design by Kimberly Martin

Cover image shows Kokopelli, Ancient Spirit Flute Player a figure that can be found on many of the Indian petroglyphs in New Mexico.

First published
Three Mile Point Publishing
June 2012

ISBN: 978-0-9848664-2-7

Library of Congress Control Number: 2012938898

Printed in the United States of America

Acknowledgments

There are many people with whom we met along the Journey and when you read this book you will know who you are. There are some great people I would like to list. The late British Master Dowser Dennis Wheatley whose book strangely came into my hands when I needed it, his daughter, author Maria Wheatley whose article in the Journal of the American Society of Dowsers triggered thoughts of geospirals.

Then there is Betty Lou Kishler my patient and dedicated partner who dowsed with me along the Journey and deftly distracted people while I dowsed sacred places, and our friend Betty Shine who read and checked my words.

Then there are a couple of spirits who dwell on the Other Side, notably my healing guide Chang who has been with me for thirty years, and a fine gentleman in spirit named Running Bear who seems to have Cosmic Records at his finger tips and somehow got me into flying astrally in time.

You are all very much appreciated.

Robert
Chaumont, NY

Contents

INTRODUCTION

Tucked away in the verdant foothills of the Sangre de Cristo Mountains of northern New Mexico there is a small, picturesque chapel where thousands of pilgrims and visitors come every year. They come to pray and be healed. They also touch the earth and fill little plastic cups and take home the precious material. Most visitors are devout believers. They call the sandy grit by the strange name "Holy Dirt." It is in fact Sacred Earth and we will show you why. It all occurs through a spiral of energy – deep within the earth.

One of the greatest mysteries facing humankind is the spiral. Is it a neat little symbol confined to pottery and pendants or does it represent deep spiritual thinking, and if this is the case, what is that thinking?

We had heard that the spiral has strange and powerful tendencies. Particularly when it takes the form of a geospiral, an earth force that can heal and attract people from a wide area. It exerts strong and beneficial forces and is the main reason I came to write this book. This work is designed both for dowsers, people who work with earth energy, would-be dowsers and general readers interested in energy forms and New Mexico.

It started in the closing days of 2008 when my partner Betty Lou and I came to Albuquerque to attend an Enneagram conference given by Father Richard Rohr. A quick trip to Santa Fe, said by tourist books to be part of the Enchanted Land resulted in us sensing the earth energy. It wrapped itself around us and penetrated our very beings and we knew we had to return. So far we have made five excursions to northern New Mexico, the last being for the entire month of October 2011.

Of course we were impressed and totally intrigued by the lonely and infinite beauty of the deserts, the towering massifs of gorgeously colored sandstone, the gorges of the Rio Grande River and the crumpled but beautiful line of the towering purple mountains known as the Sangre de Cristo Range.

But there was more: the mystical auras that surround the tell-tale ruins and rock pictures left by the prehistoric residents known as the stargazers, the people known as the Anasazi, the Ancient Ones.

There were obvious questions: Why had so many well-known people been attracted to spend time, sometimes weeks, sometimes months and sometimes years in such wayside towns as Taos and Santa Fe?

Taos came to prominence in the days of Kit Carson as a dusty little fur-trading station and in the 20th century developed into a dusty town frequented by a strange assortment of well known writers, philosophers, artists, scientists, poets, musicians, socialites, film-makers and others. Many proclaimed the place possessed a strange and obvious magnetism but no one seemed to know why. Some even suggested there might be a vortex like the ones at Sedona in Arizona, and Glastonbury in England.

We quickly discovered that a force does exist in the region and our task was to search for the source of that force and discover its benefits.

Intrigued, I started tracking the origin of this energy which both my partner Betty Lou and I could feel every time we came to northern New Mexico. However, it soon became blatantly obvious that we had tackled something that was cosmic and extremely difficult to measure with any degree of accuracy. In a nutshell, it was difficult to say what the force was exactly. Therefore we simply decided to focus upon one objective: tracking the existing energy and looking for a possible regional vortex.

While we were accomplishing this we would attempt to explain for the enjoyment and education of the reader both the historic and current environments. Dowsers have a knack of performing energy surveys of wonderfully interesting places but fail to present the background, the history, the story surrounding the energy.

What we did not know nor did we ever suspect that we would attract the attention of an old Indian shaman in spirit who would ultimately show me historic images of people and events from long ago.

This book is the record of an adventure, an exploration, a search for earth energy. They say the gold-hungry Spaniards relentlessly searched for the fabled "Golden Cities of Cibola" and went away empty-handed, but the true gold of cosmic healing was there all along but they failed to feel it. This book may assist the would-be dowser to get started and learn to dowse his own landscape. In addition it will hopefully help the reader to understand the gentle art of dowsing. It may also intrigue veteran dowsers to explore new vistas and it will certainly allow the armchair traveler to read something about northern New Mexico in a new light — the light of earth energy.

If you are a dowser you may find a geospiral in your back yard in which case you may count your blessings.

1

THE ANCIENT ART OF DOWSING

Dowsing which is part of the ancient art and science of divining had its origins thousands of years ago. In fact it is safe to say the roots of dowsing have their origins tucked away in the mists of prehistoric time.

In the Tassili n'Ajjer caves in south-east Algeria there are incredible wall paintings of wildlife, but there is also a picture of a dowser, holding a forked branch in his hands while being watched by tribal people. Carbon dating has set the paintings at over 8,000 years old.

Ancient Egyptian temples show pictographs of pharaohs with sticks resembling dowsing rods. They date 2,000 years before BCE. One of the Cairo museums contains pendulums over 1,000 years old.

Since time immemorial, dowsers have called their divining apparatus "rods." In the famous crossing of the Red (Reed) Sea Moses was instructed to use his rod. Exodus 14:16 tells the reader: *"...lift thou up thy rod, and stretch out thine hand over the sea, and divide it..."* (KJV)

That was one occasion. The second comes when the Children of Israel are thirsting in the desert. Moses is again told by God to use his rod and strike a rock. He does so and water pours forth. (Exodus 17:5/6)

Whenever the ancients required something, they simply resorted to their rods or their pendulums. They never lacked for water, never lost their way, and the divining rod always answered. Their rods and pendulums became their personal oracles and they never left home without them. Recall the words in Psalm 23: *"Thy rod and thy staff shall comfort me."*

Today, many people around the world are using dowsing instruments to tap into their higher consciousness and seek answers from the Cosmic Mind. The original and most popular use for dowsing rods was and is to discover water sources.

Dowsing has unlimited possibilities. For instance, a pendulum can be used to find directions, ask the time, check the energy of a house or an apartment you might be going to rent or purchase, discover how the weather will be on a certain date in the future, the wisdom of starting a business or economic project, enrolling in an education course and much more.

In health and welfare matters, dowsing will reveal the amount of calories on a plate of food, and determine the fat content. You can even check the nutritional content of food, and if you have a list of vitamins and minerals, you can check your own or a friend's vitamin and mineral balance in the body. Another favorite of dowsers is checking the sex of an unborn child.

Using a pendulum you can, with permission, scan a friend's body and determine a past history of surgical operations, bone breakages, organ and gland weaknesses, plus energy blockages that need to be resolved. Arthritis, a stress related disease, has a habit of originating in areas where old bone breakages occurred many years ago. Pendulums are great for tracking body and auric energies. Many naturopaths and other health professionals use pendulums for tracking the roots of physical ailments.

In metaphysics there are a number of power centers in the human body. These are known as chakras and a pendulum will tell you if they are correctly aligned or out of balance and by what percentage.

One other point, some geological exploration companies employ professional dowsers with maps to assist in finding locations for oil, gas, minerals, water, precious metals, archeological remains and even undersea treasures. This has occurred several times off the coast of Egypt, particularly Alexandria where various ruins lie at the bottom of the Mediterranean. For the most part dowsers perform their work without leaving the office. This facility is termed map dowsing and we sometimes use this technique for finding geospirals in remote locations where prolonged travel is difficult or near impossible.

THE ART OF DETECTING THE UNSEEN

So what is dowsing in a nutshell? Simply put it is the art of detecting targets either invisible or unseen. The targets are hidden beyond normal human sight.

But how does it work exactly?

The dowsing fraternity has a variety of answers. Some say it is a very fine neuromuscular reaction triggered by the Higher Self that influences pendulums and rods. Others claim it is a psychic ability but this is spurned by trueblooded dowsers. Some say the whole thing works on universal or earth energy. One point is definite: pendulums and dowsing rods do not work by themselves. There must always be a human element.

For my part, I believe dowsing is the manifestation of higher consciousness working in conjunction with the sub-conscious mind. It is the metaphysical part of our being, the intuitive sense, the sixth sense that is in tune with Universal Consciousness.

For the purpose of this book there are two instruments, the Pendulum and a pair of Dowsing Rods.

GETTING THE "RIGHT" PENDULUM

A pendulum is defined as an object suspended from a fixed support so that it swings freely back and forth under the influence of gravity. The most famous of pendulums was named after the French physicist Léon Foucault. It is a simple device conceived in 1851 to demonstrate and prove the rotation of the Earth. Most science museums have Foucault pendulums on display.

In practical terms you can use just about anything as a pendulum as long as it swings. A metal nut, key, nail or bolt tied on the end of a piece of string will create a basic pendulum. A ring, a pendant or brooch on a fine chain will do nicely. Most serious dowsers use crystals, polished stones and small brass knobs that come in various shapes and sizes. In working with maps and charts it is convenient to have a pendulum with a sharp point.

A pendulum should always feel "right" for you. Ironically, most dowsers will suggest you need to use a pendulum to find that "right" one.

CARING FOR A PENDULUM

Once you have established the right one for yourself, get a soft cloth container and keep it as you would a valuable gift. Do not allow anyone else to use it, no matter if they are the most angelic person in the world. If you think your pendulum might have been exposed to negative energy, place it on a piece of cloth and expose it to sunshine for several days. If you are in a hurry, you can wash it in sea salt water or apple cider vinegar. Both are great for cleansing pendulums from unwanted energies. Make sure your pendulum is safe for cleaning. If in doubt, use the sunshine mode.

Most pendulums come in velvet or soft cloth bags, and they should always be kept and carried in a protected place.

HOLDING THE PENDULUM

The most practical way of holding the pendulum's chain is with the forefinger and thumb of your strong hand – that's your writing hand. Some dowsers advise using the weak or non-writing hand. It's whatever works for you.

Let the pendulum hang loosely. Some people fancy longer chains, about twelve inches, others like it to be two or three inches. The fact is a shorter chain or string creates a faster response. Start with a twelve inch chain and discover your own preferred and ideal working length.

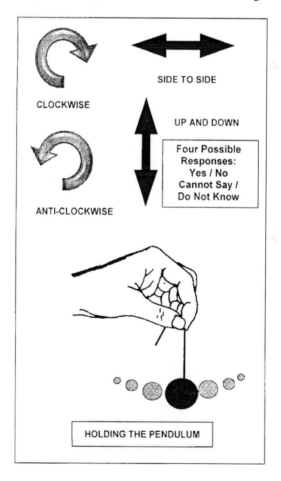

THREE OR FOUR RESPONSES

Depending upon who you ask, there can be either three or four responses obtainable from a swinging pendulum. I teach four responses, my old friend and colleague Tom Passey used to teach three. Again, it is whatever works for you.

My four responses are: YES, NO, CAN'T SAY, and DON'T KNOW. The last two responses are based on (1) your higher consciousness refusing to tell you, and (2) the higher consciousness simply does not know the answer because the question is ambiguous.

The first two responses from a pendulum are fairly straight forward. My YES is a circular clockwise movement of the pendulum, and the NO is an anti-clockwise circle. Yours may be different.

My CAN'T SAY is a straight back and forth, and my DON'T KNOW is like a shaking of the head, side to side movement. See the attached diagram.

EXERCISE – LEARNING TO SWING

To discover your responses perform the following exercise. This should be performed when you are comfortably relaxed. Never hurry dowsing. It is very much like meditation so stay cool and relaxed.

Your arm should be free, in other words not resting on a table or against your body. In fact, many dowsers suggest your arm should be a little tired, much like an arm used in automatic writing. First, give the pendulum a gentle motivating swing then generally keep your hand still after that.

(1) Address your pendulum: *"Show me a YES."* This means that when you pose a question to your pendulum, the answer will be in the affirmative. Now, when you have an affirmative response, bring the pendulum back to a slight swinging mode.

(2) This time ask your pendulum to: *"Show me a NO."*

(3) Next, do as above but address your pendulum as follows: *"Show me the response when you CAN'T SAY the answer to a question."*

(4) Finally, ask your pendulum *"Show me a DON'T KNOW response."*

Keep practicing until you get all four responses. They may be weak at first with the pendulum hardly moving, but with practice the responses become stronger. When you feel comfortable with the responses, do this simple test.

GETTING INTO THE MODE

Prepare your pendulum by allowing it to swing gently in neutral. Start a session with *"May I ask a question at this time?"* Some dowsers ask their pendulums: *"May I? Can I ? Should I? ask a question?"* It is your choice. Wait for a response and if the pendulum swings an affirmative, perform the following test.

"Is my name.......?" Pick the name of someone else. The response should be a negative.

Now use your correct name. The response should be in the affirmative.

Once you have established this, you are ready to go and dowse whatever your heart desires. However, refrain from getting excited, stressed or hurried. Pendulums and your higher consciousness are averse to fluctuating energies. But as Tom Passey advised in countless workshops: *"Practice! Practice! Practice!"* Many people neglect this point.

Experience is vital to good, effective dowsing, and experience comes through practice. If you desire to become an accomplished pianist, you must practice. Likewise if you wish to be a good skier, tennis player, mathematician, floral arranger, photographer, psychic and healer, you must practice. So it is with dowsing. Practice at every opportunity. Enjoy your trials and errors because they are all learning experiences.

USING Y-RODS AND L-RODS

If you are searching for geospirals and earth energies of any sort it is advisable to be proficient in using L-rods. We should mention a similar instrument, the Y-rod. This is a forked stick made of hazel, apple or yew or any springy wood. The Y-rod is the time-honored one used in many ancient pictures, and some traditional dowsers still use them. The Y-rod brought about the term "water-witching" and indeed its historic use has been used for finding water. The two "handles" on the upper part of the Y-rod should have a firm tension or springiness. However the L-rods are much easier to use and one L-rod can double up as a pendulum.

The L-rod looks like an L and the base forms the handle and the up-right section of the L is the pointer. L-rods come in pairs and are very popular throughout the dowsing community. In the search position the two pointing arms are parallel, and when they reach the target they either become crossed or fly apart. They range in length from about five inches to 18 inches. The longer ones are more difficult to manipulate on windy days.

Dealers and the American Society of Dowsers carry a variety of L-rods ranging from simple pieces of wire to ones with wooden and brass handles. Or you can make them yourself with a pair of wire cutters and pliers.

Find two copper coat-hangers and cut two usable pieces, perhaps 18 or 20 inches in length. Bend a length of five inches for your handle, so that the wires form an L. Next acquire two empty pen casings and slip them over the handles, then with the pliers bend the bottom of the handles so the casings do not fall off. Because the arms may be sharp slip small caps on the ends. The last thing you want is to be stabbed by your own dowsing rods.

Dowsing rods in the Search Position

Dowsing rods crossed at the Target

HOLDING THE L-RODS

There are two photos in this section showing the search position for the L-rods. The search position for using L-rods is to stand holding the handles in front of your chest with the arms pointing forward towards the horizon. Imagine you're holding two six-guns like an old time gunfighter. If there is a wind blowing reduce the aim to just below the horizon. This is where shorter L-rods excel.

CRITICAL POINTS: FOCUS AND IMAGERY

Regardless of whether you are using pendulums or rods, the operator must be able to concentrate and focus on the object which is the subject of his or her search. Visualize the object in the mind. For instance if you are looking for a geospiral, fix an image in your mind before you go into the search position. See it clearly in your mind and if any other thoughts slip in, push them out. Your subconscious mind will soon catch onto the search habit.

THE SEARCH POSITION

Hold the handles of both L-rods as described above. Walk slowly with both parallel and pointing gently down off horizontal. Focus on the object of the search. For testing purposes: search for the edges of a shadow or the underground pipes of a lawn watering system. Or have a person stand still and ask for the edge of that person's aura. The rods should cross the moment you reach the target.

ENERGY LINES TO KNOW

Geopathic: These are energy lines caused either by divisions in rock formations or by subterranean water streams. In most cases these are negative and although they do not come into geospiral research, the dowser should be aware of them. Check Käthe Bachler's book Earth Radiation.

Leylines: Sometimes called Old Tracks, these are energy lines used by the ancients for navigating from one place to another. Extensive studies have been made on the leylines in Britain and Europe. Leylines can also be found in prehistoric settlements in the United States and Central and South America.

Geodetic System: These are earth energies discovered by British master dowser, the late Guy Underwood and cover such energy flows as water lines, track lines, and something he called aquastats which are multiple lines of energy, aerial energies and geospirals. In spite of the name aquastats are not related to water.

Geospirals: Dennis Wheatley in his book The Essential Dowsing Guide describes the geospiral as one of the geodetic system's "most exotic geometric patterns." It consists of a main spiral with coils or rings in various multiples and there seems to be no fixed area of influence both horizontally and vertically. Geospiral energy as we have found in our searches carries various powers of healing and feelings of wellbeing.

USING THE L-ROD AS A PENDULUM

It is useful to prime one of your L-Rods to act as a pendulum. It can only provide Yes and No responses, but it can also act as a direction finder.

For the first part, relax with one L-rod. Allow it to point outward in a slightly down position. Ask it to "Show me a No" and watch as it swings perhaps right or left. Then ask it to "Show me a Yes" and watch it again. It should show an opposite direction. This is useful if you cannot find your pendulum.

The other use for the single rod is as a direction finder. If you are standing near an ancient monument, a mound, an old Indian encampment or a church or indeed any building, focus on a geospiral and ask your L-rod "Please point to the nearest geospiral." Then walk with both your L-rods in the search position and the rods should cross every time you pass over a line or the rings of the geospiral.

RELAX AS YOU DOWSE

It does help to get into an altered state of consciousness before using the pendulum or performing any dowsing and divining. One simple and easy way is to close your eyes and look up into the inside of your forehead for five or ten seconds then open your eyes. This action alone puts you into a light alpha state which is great for quality dowsing.

It also helps a dowser if he or she spends a few minutes every day in meditation. It raises the intuitive levels and creates a better comfort zone for the higher consciousness.

SERIOUS RESEARCH?

When you discover a geospiral or indeed any geodetic alignments, keep a detailed journal of your findings and always take photographs. Enjoy!

If you would like to get more involved in dowsing, there are a number of instruments or tools you may wish to learn about and use. The American Society of Dowsers (www.dowsers.org) has a bookstore containing a great variety of L-rods, Y-rods, bobbers and bounce rods and even the famous Cameron aurameter, and there are articles on how to use them.

Now we have discussed the basics of dowsing, let us take a look at spirals and in particular geospirals and how we found them in our target area – northern New Mexico.

SPIRALS: MESSAGES FROM SPACE?

The ancient world knew and understood the power of the spiral. It has been left to us in a multitude of ways. For instance, the Stone Age folk of the Paleolithic era in human history lived some 100,000 years ago and left all sorts of symbolism in their artwork that included spirals. Professor Flanders Petrie, one of the great Victorian archeologists found it in Egypt as did Sir Arthur Evans when he found it on scarabs on the island of Crete.

Over the years spiral designs made by the ancients have been discovered in such places as China, New Zealand, Australia, India, Scandinavia, the Pacific Islands and both North and South America.

The Neolithic folk — the New Stone Age people who lived throughout the Middle East and Europe about 10,000 years BCE left their marks on bracelets, axeheads, chisels, polishing stones and megalithic stones. For instance the Isle of Goats close to the coast of Brittany in France is the home of the impressive Gavrinnis megalithic cairn. The cairn, created about 5,500 years ago is about 60 metres in diameter and covers a passage and chamber which is lined with twenty-nine elaborately engraved stones. Many of the huge upright stones show spirals in multiple formations.

Is this an isolated case? Hardly. About the same time the Neolithics in Brittany were creating the Gavrinnis cairn, the folk in far off Ireland were building Newgrange, Knowth and Dowth. Archeologists have found they were a farming community that resided on the fertile lands of the Boyne Valley. All three contain the spiral motifs on the ancient stones. All three sites have been designated a World Heritage Site by UNESCO. They are more than just a collection of rocks and passageways or a place to watch the Heavens. Many people suggest an Ancient Temple is a more fitting classification with critical connections in astrology, spiritual and religious progression and worship. They were also the last resting place of community elders.

But as we shall see, they were not only ancient temples for adoration of the Heavens, they had gifts and powers for people who lived then. Today, they are still existant and powerful but most people ignore them. If you had a gold mine in your back yard would you ignore it?

Designers and artists have been inspired by the spiral throughout the ages. Today one sees spiral logos in churches and corporate offices. You may have flown over the Great Salt Lake in Utah and seen Robert Smithson's earthwork "Spiral Jetty."

The modern day labyrinth is an off-shoot of the ancient spiral. The ancient Celts created labyrinth carvings such as those found at Val Camonica in alpine Italy. Each major civilization and religions used the labyrinth on jewelry, shields, pottery, coats of arms, and building decorations and stones. Roof tiles that date back to the Tang Dynasty in the seventh century have been discovered in modern-day China at Xian. The ancient Celts in Britain often daubed blue wode spirals on their naked bodies to terrorize opponents on the battlefield.

The spiral can be found in minute forms as the double helix structure of DNA and in the power-fields of magnets. It can also be found in outer space, in fact the Universe is full of spirals, vast galaxies swirling round in the far reaches of the Cosmos.

The Hubble Space Telescope has produced countless pictures of spiral galaxies millions of light years away and orbiting Earth satellites have produced incredible pictures of hurricanes spiraling through the Atlantic. Incidentally one has to be out in space or over the top of a hurricane to witness the spiral effect.

Everything around us demonstrates the spiral. The tides, the seasons, the winds, particularly the enormous and frequently disturbing power of hurricanes and tornadoes. If we look at certain horned animals we can see spirals, and again in many plants particularly flowers.

Wherever you look on Planet Earth there are spirals in some form. Ever since humans learned to draw there have been spirals. So the question is, what are spirals telling us? Are they just saying "we are nice to look at?" or is there some deeper meaning?

In recent years a new phenomenon has emerged using the spiral images — crop circles. It challenges the mind and the rational ego to think that these mysterious and always perfect crop circles, many of them single and double spirals, have appeared in 58 countries throughout the world. Who or what is responsible? Are they messages? If so, what do they say? And more importantly from whom do they come. For the time being, and this book, let us simply be objective and search for spirals and their direct meaning and value for us humans.

Still, we cannot help wondering who or what embedded the Cosmic spiral symbol in the human consciousness? First of all, the spiral has a compelling shape for human consciousness. Place a black and white printed spiral on an eight by ten inch rotating cardboard form and anyone observing it for a few seconds will fall into some altered level of consciousness. Trance, they call it.

The famous Swiss psychiatrist Carl Jung considered the spiral to be an archetypal symbol that represents cosmic forces. The ancient Britons considered the spiral to be feminine and the gateway to life. Others consider the spiral as finding one's Self and Being.

There are some thinkers who believe that the spiral is embedded in our memories and perhaps our DNA because it is theorized that humanity was born out there among a billion suns and solar systems, and one of those is our galactic spiral home.

It would seem strange that this one symbol — the spiral — shows up in ancient Australian aboriginal paintings, the spiritual texts of the Hindus, Japanese rock gardens, Celtic, African and Greek art, and throughout all the eleven major religions of the world. Yet it belongs to no one and everyone. It runs deep within our lives. It is Universal, Cosmic and Infinite.

The spiral is very much like life. The cycle of birth, life and death. The continual return to Spirit, the Creator, and to be reborn again into another life cycle, not necessarily a physical cycle.

All the spirals mentioned so far are visible. One can see them, wonder at their design and perhaps ponder over their origin and existence, their infinite mystique.

But there are other spirals, spirals that are difficult if not impossible for the human eye to see. They come in all shapes and sizes and powers. They can attract and they can repel. When they come in clusters they are known as a vortex.

This phenomenon is called Geospiral. The name is derived from the Greek Gaia or Gaea meaning Earth so we get "ge" and "geo."

Geospirals have tremendous powers of creation and healing. You may have one in your back yard, and if the church down the street is very old, there's likely to be a spiral generating positive and healing energy in the aisles. Spirals have enormous powers of attraction and you may be living healthily in your home because there is a spiral energy field working for you.

THE OLD TRACK

Planet Earth is laced with phenomena called ley-lines. In 1921 an English businessman Alfred Watkins was riding his horse in Herefordshire, a county east of Wales, when he noticed that many of the foot paths and lanes seemed to connect one hilltop to another in a straight line. He subsequently coined the term "ley" because the lines passed through places whose names contained the syllables "ley, lay, lea, lee, or leigh,"

As he studied maps he noticed places in alignment. For instance churches were built in a line on old pagan or Celtic spiritual sites. "The whole thing came to me in a flash", he later told his son. He subsequently found leylines that connected standing stones, earthworks, stone monuments and circles, cairns, megaliths, barrows, and sites of ancient towns and villages.

For instance there is a leyline known as the Great Dragon Leyline that comes out of the Atlantic and runs through St. Michael's Mount in Cornwall, crosses historic places such as Glastonbury and passes through Bury St. Edmonds and disappears into the North Sea. Back in the early 1980s I walked sections of this leyline and discovered that even without dowsing rods you can sense the earth energy manifesting in your body. I could well imagine our ancient ancestors in ancient times walking along these lines as they travelled from one place to another. Leylines are like a prehistoric GPS system. But if you keep your eyes open you will observe cattle in the meadow walking along certain tracks towards their feed or barn. For the most part they all follow an invisible line and if you dowse it you are more than likely to find a leyline — the old track.

Since Watkins time there has been considerable work performed by dowsers in mapping leylines that criss-cross the country. In more recent times, the term leyline has come to be associated with spiritual and mystical theories about land forms, including Chinese feng shui, a point made by John Mitchell in his book "The New View over Atlantis."

Leylines should not be confused with another phenomenon called "geopathic stress lines," which are found in many places. These are earth energies gone awry and the good thing is they are not long, normally a few yards.

The Earth constantly transmits energy, all of it positive. As it flows upward it crosses a crack in rock formation, otherwise known as geological strata or crosses a subterranean water stream flowing over clay and certain minerals, it changes from positive to negative. There is a 180 degree phase change. While positive energy has the ability to heal, negative energy depletes the human immune system and disease moves in. If you're curious about this negative phenomena check out the classic "Earth Radiation" by Käthe Bachler.

Ley lines are entirely different and so are the objects of this book – the search for geospirals. As you will discover, leylines and geospirals are cousins and are closely related.

Although I had considerable experience in general dowsing particularly tracking dangerous geodetic stress lines and eliminating them, I really did not have any experience in the power of geospirals.

A number of questions became paramount. What power did geospirals possess and was it available? Did they emit a force so great, so beautiful over a wide area that it could attract and benefit whole cultures and various groups of people.

Like everything else in our metaphysical lives, some power somewhere seems to lead us into a place where some phenomena will occur. While we admire and respect the Spirit World I have the inclination to call what follows...

2

THE NEW MEXICO DECEPTION

How we first came to New Mexico was intriguing. We had heard that the famous Franciscan priest, Father Richrd Rohr in Albuquerque, New Mexico was presenting a four-day workshop on the Enneagram, an ancient and powerful tool for understanding ourselves. We managed to stay a couple of days afterwards and checked out the fascinating Old Town and visited the Acoma Pueblo, an ancient Indian village perched on top of a rocky, flat topped mesa.

Something about the blue skies, the richly colored landscape and the lifestyle captured our attention. Our first visit was early January. It was cold so we decided to return later in the fall for ten days with rush visits to Santa Fe, Taos, Socorro and Magdalena. It was close to this last town at a remote mountain spot that the powers got me to perform a spirit rescue at a ghost community called Kelly Mine. Eight miners who had died but their spirits had never made a safe transition called out and I helped them pass over. That was the start of the attraction – we were captured and had to discover the energies of a place they call "The Enchanted Land." At that time we had no idea why but we sensed the force was working on us. We returned home to upstate New York and made a vast collection of books, movies and notes on New Mexico – and in particular the northern area of the state. At the back of this book we have listed some of the books we collected.

The next year we visited for another ten days, continued to study the history, read numerous newspapers, visit museums and art galleries and listen to residents' stories.

We found Abiquiui, a dusty little town bordering some towering mountains with ridges and peaks that seem to reach out to Heaven with a backdrop of a beautiful turquoise lake and a panorama of desert and tumbleweed that shimmered and stretched to a distant table mountain. It was little wonder that Georgia O'Keeffe spent many of her years painting and living in the area.

We also trekked with some 5,000 people to a place called Trinity, a stretch of desert which is now called the White Sands Missile Range and is about 35 miles south-east of Socorro. It is the site where on Monday July 16th 1945 the Manhattan Project tested and detonated "The Gadget" the world's first atomic bomb. It was positioned on a 100 feet tall tower, a site that is now marked with a Ground Zero monument. The place is open to sightseers the first Saturday of April and October.

The one and only human created relic of the blast is a metal cylinder weighing 214 tons which was designed to contain the TNT explosion if the chain reaction failed to materialize. Named Jumbo and positioned 800 yards from ground zero the experts estimated it would be completely vaporized if the atomic explosion was successful. Well, two large chunks of it remain. The main part is at the Trinity Site and you can walk through it while a small chunk is displayed in the square at the old cattle and mining town of Socorro thirty miles away. For sensitives and people who practice psychometry it contains a visible record of the explosion well over six decades later.

In Socorro we placed our hands on the Jumbo relic and both Betty Lou and I felt the violence of that day in July 1945. If one is patient the psychometrist practitioner can view Jumbo being carried on a railway at snail's pace, watch it being transferred to 64-wheeled trailer and hauled across the desert.

The Socorro relic shows through psychometry the explosion and it is strange, the eery silence that descends on the desert. Not a thing moves. No dust, no birds, no clouds. Nothing. Just total quiet. Eventually the Jumbo relic provides images of helmeted workers investigating the site. But I feel it is that total silence, images of the world standing still that is one of the most powerful psychic events I have ever witnessed. It was better than any movie of the event.

THE REGION OF INTEREST

Sitting at home by the shores of Chaumont Bay and Lake Ontario we often wondered why so many people, so many cultures, so many individuals – including us — were attracted to New Mexico.

Many people like the British author D.H. Lawrence, the socialite Mabel Dodge Luhan, artist Georgia O'Keeffe, Swiss psychiatrist Carl Jung and film-maker Dennis Hopper, all frequently claimed there was an attraction, a magnetism that pulls one to the region.

It started almost a thousand years ago with the great migration of the Native Indians who were drawn to create more pueblos in the region than anywhere else in the world. Then there were the hippies who swarmed there in 1969 seeking their Utopia, only to be disillusioned at not finding it and publicly announcing the place was "Dead. Stay away."

Yes, the place has a memorable beauty. Towering, multi colored mountain ridges and exquisite rocky mesas, desert plains and great forests, snow-capped mountains of the Sangre de Cristo Range, countless dry creeks called arroyos, and the remains of a once great and mighty river that that flows weakly through a 600 foot gorge. Its name? The Rio Grande.

The region of our interest was north of Albuquerque in the valley of the Rio Grande which curves and streches north to the Colorado border . The main communities are Santa Fe the capital of New Mexico, Espanola, Taos, Chimayó, Angelfire and Los Alamos. The tourist fraternity promotes the region as the Enchanted Circle, a sort of circular drive round and through the beautiful purple-hazed mountains.

But we were searching for something deeper than visual beauty. As we studied the books, the photographs and videos and pondered the writings of the people who lived and visited the region, we kept returning to that one word, the one quality – magnetism! Somehow we realized that we were being called, being attracted to that Enchanted Land. As dowsers we felt the urge to explore.

One day my spirit friends were extremely noncommittal when they suggested: "Take your pendulums, dowsing rods and an open mind and it will be shown unto you."

At this point we had no idea of why we were going, in fact we we had no knowledge of the much bandied word magnetism, let alone geospirals. Anyway, we decided to rent a neat little condo called Santerra in downtown Taos for the entire month of October 2011. In order to have our own transportation we would drive from our starting off point at Pemberton, New Jersey to Taos. A distance of 2,000 miles, we estimated we could drive 500 miles a day and stay at places along Interstate 70.

A lot of people openly expressed the view that we were entirely mad. "People in their seventies don't do that sort of thing," a well-meaning friend once announced. "Have you any idea why you are doing this?"

At that point we simply talked about the beauty of the mountain vistas, the rivers and deserts because we thought people would not understand if we announced we were searching for an energy, a magnetism that draws people. It's bad enough telling people we are into metaphysics, mysticism and dowsing. Their eyes will adopt a strange haziness, then suddenly realizing you are speaking the truth, their faces react in sheer alarm. You imagine they are going to rush out collect firewood to burn you at the stake. So we just talked about the beauty of the land and the old world comforts of a little condo in Taos. But frankly at this point just a couple of weeks before our departure, we had no idea for what our target might be. Then it happened.

MASTER DOWSER DENNIS WHEATLEY

An oldish copy of the Journal of the American Society of Dowsers kept on coming into my line of vision. I picked it up and my eyes flicked to an article by an English lady, Maria Wheatley. Ms. Wheatley is an expert on Avebury, a specialist in earth mysteries and she teaches past life regression, reflexology and dowsing part time at Swindon College in England. In her article she mentioned the phenomena of an earth force called "geospiral" and the work done on it by her father and master dowser, the late Dennis Wheatley who lived in Swindon.

Her father, a world-authority on the geodetic system of earth energies taught Maria how to locate and dowse these powerful earth energies in the English landscape particularly in and around Avebury. This is the site of a large henge, a prehistoric architectural structure that dates back 5,000 years. It outdates Stonehenge which is 20 miles to the south.

Somehow I felt I needed to know about geospirals, so I emailed her.

Maria told me there is a good introduction to geospirals in her father's book "The Essential Dowsing Guide." It arrived from England a few days before we were scheduled to leave for our jumping off spot, Pemberton, New Jersey so I tossed it into my case and didn't see it again until the first night stop at a motel near Coloumbus Ohio.

After dinner, a spirit voice urged: "Pick up the Wheatley book.

" I did and promptly devoured the information on geospirals, triple leylines and a host of other interesting material.

According to Wheatley, a geospiral is one of the geodetic system's "most exotic geometric patterns." A main spiral will comprise coils of energy in multiples of seven up to a maximum of forty-nine. It can be either single or double rings that form the geospirals. They are affected at different times by the moon, noticeably at full and new moons.

Wheatley writes there are many such geospirals on sacred places throughout the world particularly where there are ancient stones or mounds.

For some time I had the feeling that our friends in Spirit were prodding and pushing me to do things, such as reading Maria's article in the Dowsers' Journal. Send for a copy of Dennis Wheatley's book. All may have been a coincidence, but what happened next in Columbus was more than just a coincidence.

Next day we planned to drive along Interstate 70, and stay the night in St. Louis, the place where the Missouri joins the great Mississipi river.

It was in the end section of the book where Dennis writes about a place called the Monks Mound that my full attention was suddenly sparked. The Monks Mound at Cahokia, Illinois, said the author, is the largest prehistoric earthwork construction in the world and nearby is a circle of cedar poles known as the "Woodhenge" of America.

28

In the book Dennis instructs the reader: "Dowse this for a geospiral presence and check if the circle is set by an earth energy 'halo' comprising three parallel hairlines.

"Aren't we going through Illinois?" asked Betty Lou.

I thumbed the map. "Our next night stop is St. Louis, Missouri and Cahokia in Illinnois is just before we cross the Mississippi. It's right on our path."

We were both amazed at this turn of events. "What a strange coincidence," I muttered.

"Spirits at work," she commented drily.

THE CAHOKIA EXPERIENCE

Cahokia is a fascinating complex of earth mounds. In its heyday it was a city larger than London in the 13th century. Covering more than 2,000 acres, archeologists say it was the most sophisticated prehistoric Native Indian civilization north of Mexico. It is best known for the large man-made earthen structures which would had dwarfed the pyramids of Egypt.

Cahokia was inhabited from about 600 to 1400 A.D. Built by ancient peoples known as the Mound Builders, Cahokia's original population stood at about 1,000 until the 11th century when it suddenly expanded to as many as 100,000. Inhabitants lived in homes that were arranged in rows around open plazas. Agricultural farms and small villages in the suburban area supplied the city which became a center for trading with other tribes.

The Cahokians were known to have traded with other tribes living as far away as the Great Lakes. It is surprising then that as merchants and traders they possessed no writing skills. One wonders how they kept track of their tradings. The ancient Sumerians in the Middle East developed Cuneiform, a writing system whose wedge-shaped strokes allowed numbers and quantities to be kept.

The ancient Cahokians built more than 120 earthen mounds of which 109 have been recorded and 68 are preserved within the site. While some are just small heaps, others are magnificent earthworks reaching 100 feet into the sky. The ancients transported the soil on their backs in baskets to the building sites. An estimated 50 million cubic feet of earth was moved for the construction of the mounds, leaving large depressions called barrow pits, which can still be seen in the area.

The largest earthwork is called Monks Mound and it holds the title of the largest prehistoric earthen mound in North America. Measuring 1,000 feet long, 800 feet wide it was comprised of four terraces, each one probably added at different times. An estimated 22 million cubic feet of earth was used to build the mound on which archeologists figure the principal ruler lived and the seat of government existed.

The mound received its name from the French Trappist monks who lived nearby in the early 1800s. Time and mankind have caused parts of the Monks' Mound to be eroded so that the original size is now uncertain.

And yes, there is mystery surrounding Cahokia. A positively thriving city and trading center with a large population suddenly falls into decline in 1200 A.D. and within two centuries the entire metropolis is totally abandoned.

Why? Theories abound. Perhaps climate changes, disease, drought, invasion. As we shall see in our journey, another great prehistoric Indian complex was dying at the same time, 1,200 miles away.

There's another fascinating mystery.

Archeologists continue to be puzzled by the fact that there are no legends, records, nor mention of the once great metro city of Cahokia in the lore of other local tribes, including the Osage, Omaha, Ponca and Quapaw nations. Some experts believe that this strange silence indicates something very negative occurred at Cahokia and the other tribes simply want to forget.

But many people including Native Americans and metaphysical groups consider the Cahokia site to be sacred. They say it is a source of powerful earth energy. Incidentally Cahokia is one of only 21 World Heritage Sites existing in the United States.

So we arrived mid-afternoon on a sunny day in late September, gathered a bundle of information from the large Information Center and Betty Lou immediately climbed the long column of steps scaling the great Monks' Mound. The steps are to stop people otherwise climbing the grass covered mound and causing further erosion.

My rods indicated a triple leyline coming across the Mississippi and running along the axis of the Mound. There was no indication of a geospiral and not much energy coming from the leyline either. Initially I was disappointed.

Where was the Woodhenge mentioned by Dennis Wheatley?

We had to ask for directions. A five minute drive along the Collinsville Road brought it into sight. It is called "Woodhenge" after Britain's "Stonehenge." This Cahokian structure performed much the same task as an astronomical observatory and calculator in other words the Cahokians were stargazers.

The henge comprises a large circle of cedar poles standing about 20 feet tall. The placement of the posts mark the summer and winter solstices and the spring and autumn equinoxes. In reality the posts are a calendar, similar to the stone equivalent of Stonehenge on Salisbury Plain in England.

The first of the five circles was discovered accidentally in 1961 by Dr. Warren Wittry for the Illinois State Museum. It was 410 feet in diameter and contained 28 posts. Later four more circles were discovered with varying numbers of poles. The original posts were made of red cedar considered sacred to the Indians. The reconstructed one has 48 post holes although not all are filled. All visible indications are that it served as a practical and spiritual calendar but as we were to find out it has powers that dowser Dennis Wheatley in far off England sensed and wrote about. A geospiral!

Armed with two L-rods I started at the east side of the outer ring, focused on earth energy and instantly the rods crossed indicating a line. It was brief and the rods opened again as I moved on. At seven paces they crossed again and then quickly reopened. This occurred at every seven paces until I reached the center pole.

As I stood by the center pole, I could feel the earth energy coming into my feet like a pins and needles sensation. The energy swirled up my legs and body until it reached my head. For a few seconds I felt dizzy and clung to the center pole.

"Gaia! It is Gaia sharing her energy with you," whispered Chang. "In the old days sick people were brought here and tied to the stake or placed around the pole and after a few hours they were cured of their sickness."

"Why do I get images of people dying where I am standing?"

"True. Some people — the elders — were allowed to cross into the Other World at this particular point. They were carried on Gaia's earth energy. They say that their ancestors who had become angels would come and carry them up or down."

"Up or down?" I remarked. "I had heard that all Indians believe the departed join their ancestors in the earth."

"That was a sharp conflict that developed with the shamans," Chang said. "Tradition called for departing spirits to join the ancestors in the earth, but one of the Cahokia elders had a vision which showed departing spirits joining ancestors at the hunting grounds in the sky. It created an intense rift that haunted the Cahokians in their finals years here."

"What about the astronomical aspects of this woodhenge?"

"It was aligned both to sun and moon energies. The circle proved to be more powerful at certain points of the lunar cycle. Today, September 28th 2011 there is a new moon and the energy is very much at full strength today."

"My body feels distinctly energized," I said..

Several times I walked the circle checking the lines at seven paces holding the rods at the four feet level.

"Hold your rods at the six feet level and walk the radius again," advised Chang.

"The lines are not quite the same," I told Chang. "They are not in the same place and the energy is moving counter-clockwise."

"The geospiral has two energy patterns each counter to the other, he said. 'They form an aerial dome."

"How high."

"Twenty-one of your feet," said Chang easily. "At least today."

"What is that supposed to mean?"

"The dome changes both in height and power according to Cosmic influences. It is very much like the tides of the sea, they come and go twice a day. Well, here they have astral tides which change every fourteen and twenty-eight days. The energy changes direction." Chang stared at me. "Bob, you feel more energized?"

"Absolutely!" I said. Even as I stood there one could feel the earth energy coming into my feet and up my legs until it flowed through my entire body. Pleasant and relaxing.

"Well, you are receiving earth energy," said Chang. "It's rebalancing your body energies with blue and red light. Welcome to your first geospiral."

"It's like a vortex," I said.

"You could call it that. The shamans or medicine men used to come here, pray and recharge their bodily healing reservoirs then go off and give hands-on healing to those in the community who were sick. And of course, it worked."

"Why didn't they bring the sick to Woodhenge?"

"People were afraid of bad spirits," said Chang, "besides, the shamans needed to appear in charge. It was a power thing, as you might say. They did bring novices here when they were ready."

Then I remembered something. Leylines! The rods detected two, one coming from across the woods and the Mississippi, and another coming from the Monks Mound. Neither of them were rod-twisters, in other words, very strong.

Dennis Wheatley had said in his book that Woodhenge near Stonehenge in Wiltshire, England is located over a blind spring with its characteristic geospiral pattern. On Cahokia he advised to check if the circle of cedar poles at Cahokia is likewise located.

A blind spring is an underground dome of rock holding down pressurized water. It is the force that usually generates a geospiral above although as we found later, geospirals can exist without a blind spring and some geospirals can come up from beneath water as in a lake.

It was easy to detect the blind spring at Woodhenge but its size is something else. There are strong indications that Cahokia was built on a rock platform quite deep underground. At Woodhenge the rock dome starts at 71 feet and is over 20 feet thick. The blind spring will be the cause of streams as one nears the banks of the river.

While I moved around and took some photographs, Chang watched and suddenly pointed upwards. I was standing right by the center pole at Woodhenge. As I looked up, the beautiful wispy clouds parted and allowed the top of the sacred cedar post to be enveloped by pure blue sky. It was an omen? If so, for what?

"Now you have completed your training in geospirals," said Chang. "It was necessary for you to experience this before reaching New Mexico."

"Why? What's the problem there?" I asked. But there was no reply. The old Chinese doctor had moved on. I sensed the old Master Dowser Dennis Wheatley had been watching us all along because I heard a distinctly English voice say: "Don't forget to dowse the chapel at Chimayó."

Later while on our way across the Mississippi to St. Louis Chang reappeared and I asked how he knew things that occurred eight centuries ago.

"All universal information is available to one who asks," he said with a chuckle.

"Who did you ask?"

"While you were at Cahokia, particularly at Woodhenge, there was the spirit of an ancient shaman following and watching us. He answered your question."

Suddenly, I was alert. "The spirits of shamans are still around after eight centuries?"

"They call themselves guardians. Each of the major geospirals and vortexes have spirit guardians," said Chang. "That is why some people are afraid to go near them. The shamans still hold their powers."

"That's interesting," I thought to myself. "The search for vortices and geospirals in New Mexico is going to be very interesting."

3

THE ANASAZI STAR GAZERS

Our search for energy phenomena — a vortex and geospirals — has to start in the wild and barren desert lands of north-west New Mexico where is a place called the Four Corners because it is where four states come together. It is the only place in the United States where you can have a foot in New Mexico, another in Colorado, and one hand in Arizona and the other in Utah. Just don't try this if your body is a bit creaky.

From the Four Corners if we head across the desert we find the historic remains of a great civilization. Named Chaco Canyon it is miles from anywhere. It sits at the end of a rough road and the nearest gas station is 70 miles away.

These days the land in and around the Canyon is a territory of extremes. High temperatures of 120 degrees under a blazing summer sun and frigid temperatures under the bitter wind-swept snows of winter. But the scenery is spectacular and it includes spacious white deserts dotted with countless tumbleweeds and cedar bushes with backdrops of multi-colored mountains, many flat capped rock risings called mesas, gorges with perilous but colorful rock faces opening up to vistas of perfectly blue skies. The artist and the traveler gets the impression that God must have been delighted in creating such a wild barbaric but beautiful place. The region in its infinite beauty is taunting and inviting but to the unwary traveler it can be dangerous if not lethal.

The desert lands were not always like this. If you had come this way 1,000 years ago you would have found lush vegetation, great stands of timber mostly pine, large animals such as deer, bison and elk wandering besides free running rivers. In prehistoric times the ancestral fathers, the hunter-gatherers came down from the north, some say across the land bridge at Bering between Asia and Alaska. Many moved on southward through the continent and became known as the Aztecs, Mayans and Incas.

But in 700 A.D. the Native Indians started to settle in the area in and around Chaco Canyon. As the years passed the elders envisioned and created an enormous commune, an alliance of hamlets, villages and towns, inter-connected by a hundreds of miles of roads that became known as the Chaco civilization. These Native Indian farmers and hunters, united through economic and religious cords lived and worked together over seven centuries to build a viable region that flourished as a wonderful and awe-inspiring region for another two centuries.

In those days only a few low gorges and mesas interrupted the general flatness of the plains which for the most part were arable. Crops were basically corn and squash and farmers gathered many wild plant foods while hunters searched for deer, pronghorn antelope, jackrabbits, prairie dogs and gathered wild turkey eggs. Anthroplogist David E. Stuart describes their incredible lifestyle in great detail in his book "Anasazi America."

This Native Indian culture existed for seven centuries but Chaco peaked as a major center of Puebloan culture between 850 and 1250 A.D.

Archeologists say these people just were not the wild scalp-hunting Indians depicted by Hollywood but they were tall, athletic, highly intelligent and cosmically inclined. They knew and understood the celestial skies better than most people today.

Chacoan architects designed and built buildings according to the sun, moon and the stars along with roads based on compass directions. These highways stretched for hundreds of miles and serviced farms and smaller community centers.

Some cynics might claim these aspects as coincidences but recent findings proved that a thousand years ago the Chacoans were astronomers. This was discovered in 1977 when Anna Sofaer was working on a field project on top of the impressive Fajada Butte at Chaco.

A remarkable phenomenon occurred: a single shaft of sunlight perfectly passed between two rock monoliths and appearing like a sun dagger it illuminated some petroglyphs. This prompted return visits to conduct observations. Ms. Sofaer discovered that at the winter solstice the same "sun dagger" sliced through a smaller petroglyph nearby and two parallel daggers framed the larger spiral at the spring and fall equinoxes. The petroglyphs were spirals and the sun dagger was spot on.

The find was sensational. It triggered years of intense investigation plus a flurry of controversy with many narrow minded academics scoffing at the theory. They quickly pointed out that the sun was not known in Anasazi petroglyphic art as a spiral. Others more in tune with Cosmic teachings pointed out that the spiral represented the Universe, the Cosmos and was therefore quite appropriate.

Anna Sofaer's work suggested that Chaco was more of a pilgrimage site for the region, rather than a residential community. This theory was reinforced as archeologists mapped 37 kivas at Pueblo Bonito at Chaco. A kiva is generally known as a spiritual place, more like a church, chapel, synagogue or temple. It was a gathering place for the elders and the shamans. There is some suggestion that the large number of kiva-shaped buildings indicated they were used for storage vats or containers for corn and water.

There is an immense sadness in this story. Fajada Butte resembles a pyramid 480 feet above Chaco Canyon level floor. The revelation that it was a prehistoric site resembling Britian's Stonehenge attracted tourists and researchers in record numbers and they all climbed the butte's steep trail, scrambling up through a staircase of loose gravel and rocks to the site itself. In 1982 the National Park Service declared the Butte off limits to all but scientific researchers.

But the damage had been done. The trail had become so worn and deep by a pathway that created a gutter, the sudden, harsh summer storms did the rest and created instability among the ancient rocks. In 1989 disaster struck Fajda Butte. The base of stone monoliths was suffering from erosion and the great rocks started to slip and the ancient technology that had created a complex astronomical calendar was gone. The sun dagger that had faithfully recorded astronomical observations for centuries was destroyed in just twelve years. The dynamic proof that the Chacoans were very much the star gazers and energy watchers was now extinct.

The sun dagger was recorded on film. Broadcast nationally on PBS it was entitled "The Mystery of Chaco Canyon" and narrated by Robert Redford.

There is evidence that the Chacoans were not just stargazers they were experts in measuring energy. Many of the kivas at Chaco contain geospiral energy centers and how else would they have been able to construct buildings and roads that directly pointed north if they did not have a compass or a dowsing rod. Chances are they had both.

AN EMPIRE TOO BIG

A culture is much like an empire and the weak point about empires is they cannot sustain change whether that might come in the shape of war, societal betterment, extended regions or environmental shifts. Let us look at the Chaco culture.

It is said that in the one hundred years before 1200 A.D. the entire community complex of farms and smaller centers covered several hundred square miles. The Anasazi used the pine trees for their large and small buildings and also to support the roofs of the kivas, the spiritual centers. They also used wood for heating with the consequence the forest lands disappeared and with them the big game animals, the deer, bison and elk.

The environment suffered drastic changes and the life-supporting rains became fewer with the consequence crops withered and rivers and creeks dwindled. Severe droughts struck the region and they sometimes lasted for years.

With food supplies dwindling people died from starvation. Researchers say families were lucky if one in five new born children reached their first birthdays. In desperation families deserted the farms and moved towards the valley of the the Rio Grande and the foothills of the Sangre de Cristo Mountains. In a mere 40 years the Indian culture that had dominated Chaco Canyon for centuries was gone.

But Chaco Canyon is a special place and is still revered and respected today as part of the sacred homeland of Pueblo Indian peoples of New Mexico, the Hopi Indians of Arizona, and the Navajo Indians of the Southwest. It is still remote and isolated and for many years its existence baffled researchers. Was the magnetic power that had attracted the Anasazi in the first place also dead? Hardly, because that energy still exists at Chaco today.

Let us look at the 37 kivas built at Chaco Canyon. Many of them no longer exist but the ones that do, several have one distinct power – geospirals!

To the Native Indians a kiva was more than just a spiritual gathering place for exchanging thoughts and participating in ceremonies. It was the gateway to the Other World, the place of their ancestors, the Spirit World and it was here that the spirits would impart advice to the shamans and medicine men.

Somewhere in each Kiva there was a sipapu, a small hole measuring 12 to 18 inches in diameter. This was the gateway, the entrance, the portal to and from the Other World. The Anasazi believed the spirits of their ancestors known as kachinas would emerge from the underworld to join the living in various ceremonies and rituals. It seems they were always led by a locust playing a flute, a symbol often displayed in petroglyphs.

The shamans or medicine men, the priests of the Anasazi, would lead the ceremony normally in the evening. They would be entranced with the help of hallucinatory herbs and plants, usually the cactus-based peyote taken in the form of tea. People attending the event would use natural tobacco and incense made from the resins of cedar, sage and pine. These were aids in saying prayers and chanting which would often continue well through the night.

The people attending would form a circle round the sipapu and the shaman conducted the service. Prayers would request help from various powers for the health of loved ones, resolution of family or neighbor conflicts, enhance intuitive powers particularly in hunting and farming of crops. Prayers were also said for the safety and success of roadmen — merchants – who traded with tribes as far north as the Great Lakes, California and down into Mexico.

The sipapus or spirit portals at Chaco Canyon and other Native Indian settlements are still powerful today, even though they might appear inactive to the tourist or casual observer.

In modern day America, the sipapu was the altar, the focal point of a spiritual ceremony and the circle around it was much like the prayer, healing and spiritual development circles held in religious services, particularly in spiritualism.

For the dowser, the sipapu is often the site of a geospiral. The Anasazi not only knew the ways of the sun, the moon and the stars, they were well aware of the powers of the earth, the gifts that come from Gaia and the Underworld. Geospirals are gifts of the Spirit of the Earth and as the Anasazi discovered, they possess the powers of healing, energizing, and spirit communication. As we were to later discover in our quest, spirits ride the energies of the geospirals.

People who are studying the Anasazi and geospirals can explore the energies of these ancient people and Chaco Canyon by performing map and photo dowsing.

EXERCISE : Acquire a good map or photos of Chaco Canyon particularly any graphics of the Great House at Pueblo Bonito and using a pendulum search for geospirals. As in map reading it is useful to have a pendulum with a sharp point. Alternatively, use a fine pen, pencil or pointer and prime the pendulum to respond to that instrument. Look for geospirals and leylines and make a list of where you find them. Ask to be shown the Area of Influence of a particular geospiral usually in yards or meters. If you discover a set of closely aligned geospirals check their joint Area of Influence which may be several miles, in which case you might be researching a vortex. If possible travel to the area and conduct physical research on the spot.

THE CAVE DWELLERS AT BANDELIER

There are the remains of another ancient Native Indian community aligned with cosmic energies and much easier to access than Chaco Canyon. It's called the Bandelier National Monument. This national park covering 33,000 acres is situated in a rugged but spectacular and beautiful canyon and flanked by amazing mesas. The park which is easily accessible by good roads is situated about 40 miles north-east of Santa Fe.

Bandelier's human history started over 10,000 years ago when nomadic hunter-gatherers, off-shoots of the Anasazi, followed migrating wildlife across the mesas and canyons. While the Anasazi left no written words or documents, the inhabitants of this community left a series of beautiful rock inscriptions — petroglyphs!

By 1150 A.D. the Pueblo people began to build more permanent settlements and farm the earth. In the park at Frijoles Canyon there are a number of ancestral pueblo homes, spiritual kivas, rock paintings and petroglyphs. Some of the original structures were built on the narrow canyon floor, but later as danger from marauding bands of Indians became very clear they developed caves in the soft stone of the canyon walls. When attacks ultimately came, the residents climbed ladders into the safety of the caves and quickly pulled the ladders after them. Known as "cavates" the caves were produced by natural voids in the volcanic tuff of the canyon walls and systematically enlarged by carving and digging. The fact they are still there today demonstrates the worthiness of cave habitation.

At the central plaza there existed a large circular community called Tyuonyi. Keres speaking Indians say the name means a place of meeting or treaty. Some of the buildings go up three stories and the entire pueblo complex in its heyday contained about 400 rooms. Such Pueblo Indians whether dwelling on the plain or in the cliffs used adobe, that is sun-dried bricks to build their homes.

There are three kivas on the plaza each one underground and accessed by ladders but only one has been developed for viewing. Although one can walk on a strict path through Tyuoni, the three kivas are strangely devoid of geospirals.

A short distance away there is a stream called the Rito de los Frijoles which flows through the canyon and it parallels a strong leyline a short distance away. The dowsing rods showed several underground springs contributing to the stream.

Where did the spirits talk at Frijoles Canyon? A short distance away from Tyuonyi there is what is called the "Big Kiva." Here a major geospiral that appears like a double helix radiates positive energy about seventy-five yards in any direction. The interior of the kiva is off limits but one can stand on the path by the top of the walls and feel the energy. Most visitors only spend a couple of minutes with tour guides and they may or may not feel the healing energies emanating from this phenomenon. Experience has shown exposure lasting 15 to 30 minutes is required for any real healing. If you are a dowser with a pendulum, check to see what exposure you need for this particular geospiral or indeed any geospiral. They have different powers and effects on people.

While kivas today are for the most part appearing like expanded wells, in actual practice they were covered by a strong roof made of wood and earth and cemented with a mud-mortar mix. This reinforcement allowed people to walk on the roof. At Big Kiva the roof was supported by six wooden pillars. Entry was gained via a ladder and flickering torches offered the only lights inside.

Unlike the geospiral at Cahokia's Woodhenge the big kiva was used as a discussion center where important decisions were made and knowledge and teachings from the elders and shamans were shared. At times of spiritual ceremonies the kiva with its geospiral powers would have been used for healing and communication with spirits, notably the ancestors. This was later confirmed in an interview I did with a Native Indian shaman in spirit.

There is a completely rebuilt kiva at the Ceremonial Cave at Bandelier National Monument and yes, it does have a geospiral and it is on a leyline.

As I sat and wondered about Bandelier and Chaco, several things came to mind. In spite of their apparent knowledge of the sun, moon and celestial cycles, they were devoid of any real technology. For instance the wheel was completely unknown. Before the arrival of the Europeans in 1540 the Native Indians did not have horses, mules, oxen and most other beasts of burden used in other parts of the world. The Spaniards also introduced the two and four wheeled carts to the Pueblo Indians.

As a result, the early Indians never developed the wheel, though they were aware of its principle. For small items they used dog-and sled transport and if objects were too heavy they either carried or abandoned them.

Because just like the Cahokians and the Chacoans something made the Bandelier people suddenly abandon their seemingly very secure cliff dwellings and move to the environmentally richer and rewarding lands of the Rio Grande valley. By 1550 the Ancestral Pueblo people at Bandelier had moved from their homes to pueblos along the Rio Grande know as Cochiti, San Felipe, San Ildefonso, Santa Clara and Santo Domingo. Their descendants can be found in these pueblos today.

What was the cause of this drift to the valley of the Rio Grande? Over-population? Disease? Drought? Lack of wild animals to hunt? All things considered, it could have been the harsh reality of drought. But there seemed to be something deeper. I resolved to find out by asking the spirits. Chang my healing spirit guide announced one day that an old shaman with many years in spirit would meet me when I least expected it. That left me wondering when.

THE MIGRATION TO THE RIO GRANDE

As most people of the present age are aware it is sometimes traumatic to pull up roots and move to greener pastures. The Anasazi families and communities did it over a period of years and this raises another question: if they were so spiritually tied through the kivas and the portals to the Spirit World, how did they expect to find new places, new portals, new sipapus?

The theory is that before the time arrived for the community to move, shamans reconnoitered the lands in and around the the Rio Grande and in the foothills of the Sangre de Cristo Mountains. Some tribal people had moved earlier. For instance, the Tewa-speaking tribe that was to become known as the Taos Pueblo sensed impending doom moved and acquired land in the mountain areas and their shamans found several important geospirals as we shall see.

The highest summit in New Mexico is Wheeler Peak with an elevation of over 13,000 feet close to a place called Taos, although there are higher peaks in the Sangre Range in Colorado. In New Mexico the timberline – the region where trees stop growing — is unusually high, well over 12,000 feet in some places. There are no permanent snowfields or glaciers in this New Mexican range.

It is in the shadow of these mountains and by the healthy and steady flow of the Rio Grande with its various tributaries that the descendants of Chaco Canyon created their new pueblos. Archeologists tell us that by the end of the 1300s there were at least 150 pueblos, thirty of them major villages thriving in the foothills of the Sangre de Cristos Mountains, all with access to the life sustaining tributaries of the Rio Grande. The tribal shamans knew there was energy, cosmic energy, earth energy in the region and pueblos were sited according to earthly emissions.

Life for the ancients was good. They hunted for deer, antelope, elk, bear, rabbits and turkeys in the grasslands and foothills of the mountains where junipers and piñons flourished and fished in the waterways flanked by cottonwoods and willows.

THE COMING OF THE SPANIARDS AND RELIGION

But there were others who were attracted to the Land of Enchantment. The Spaniards! Spain had successfully freed the Iberian peninsula from the Muslim Moors after nearly 800 years of occupation and there was an urgent need for gold to finance visions of an expanded and powerful Spanish Empire.

Francisco Vasquez de Coronado, the Conquistador and Explorer came north in 1540 from Mexico with an expedition consisting of 340 Spaniards, 300 Indians, 1,000 horses, over 1,000 slaves and six swivel cannons indicating that the team was prepared for violence. Their orders from Spain was to search for the legendary Seven Golden Cities of Cíbola and in building a new empire it was an opportunity to convert the Indians who were seen as pagans and heathens into Spanish Catholicism.

Coronado arrived at Zuni Pueblo and found one of the Anasazi groups that had gone west in what was to become the State of New Mexico. Instead of gold they found precious turquoise and silver but that did not satisfy Coronado who had strict orders to find gold. He searched along the Rio Grande and eventually discovered the Grand

Canyon then unhappily returned to Mexico virtually empty handed. As one shaman suggested: "They had heard that the houses of Cibola were built of gold. In actuality what they should have searched for the Source of the Gods – Heaven."

But the Spanish occupation in the latter years of the 16th century left a ghastly legacy — smallpox, syphilis, measles and whooping cough. The fragile immune systems of the Native Indians failed to protect and thousands died in the pueblos. Some pueblos were completely wiped out particularly in the area of what was to be Santa Fe.

The healing powers of the kivas with their geospirals failed to keep up with the dying. The kivas quickly became clogged with the sick and many sick people lacked the energy to drag themselves to the spiritual centers. The killing diseases were not selective — shamans, elders as well as ordinary puebloeans were stricken by the scourge.

In addition, the Spaniards made extensive labor demands on the pueblos taking healthy Indians away to serve as slaves — tasks from which few ever returned.

Perhaps the greatest audacity came when Spaniards and other Europeans of that era announced their firm belief that the diseases inherited from Europe were acts of God being cast on their behalf. One settler proclaimed while speaking about the deaths of Native Americans: "Their enterprise failed for it pleased God to affect these Indians with such a deadly sickness that out of every 1000 over 950 of them died and many of them lay rotting above the ground for lack of burial."

No one really knows how many Native Indians died and statistics contained in the works of Fray Alonso de Benavides, a Portugese Franciscan missionary who wrote historical documents covering the 17th century have been largely discredited.

But one thing is certain the Indians were at first friendly but the conduct of the Spaniards soon provoked hostility and resistance which was put down with 100 prisoners who had surrendered being burnt at the stake or shot as they attempted to escape. Many other agitators and protesters were butchered in various ways by the Spaniards.

In 1630 there were over 50 friars administering to some 60,000 Indians living in 90 surviving pueblos. They lived and were governed by 25 mission jurisdictions a fact that did nothing but stir up revenge and violence among the descendants of the Anasazi. For the next fifty years there were serious outbreaks of violence between the Spanish administration, Spanish settlers and the Pueblo Indians.

In August 1680 it culminated in a massive retaliation by the Indians. Nearly 400 Spaniards were killed including two-thirds of the 33 missionaries. The Spanish Governor and every Spaniard in the territory were forced to withdraw to Mexico and the Indians watched them go.

The Pueblo Indians were left alone for a dozen years but there was no peace. The pueblos were frequently attacked by neighboring Navajos, Apaches and Comanches.

Then in the late 1600s Spanish civilization returned to Santa Fe and the region.

Historians often wonder what was it that attracted the Spaniards and the missionaries to return to the land that was to become New Mexico. The legend of cities of gold had long been shot down. There were no big trading opportunities and the land with its mountains and deserts was generally inhospitable. What was the magnetism that demanded the Spaniards stay and colonize this troublesome province of Spain?

As the Indian population decreased due to sickness, poverty and the brutality of slavery so the pueblos became deserted and decreased in numbers. Sharp conflict arose between the old natural mystical ways of their ancestors and the new Christian religion brought by the Spaniards.

The gift to the Pueblo Indians was the brutal Spanish Inquisition. It was established in New Mexico territory in 1626 where it terrorized the Native Indians. In many pueblos, churches were built on spots considered sacred to the Pueblo Indians. Preachers in the pulpits declared that the old ways, the Kachinas were evil as were the sipapus in the kivas. The Catholic priests branded them as "witchcraft" and "enemies of God."

One wonders if the holy missionaries knew what they were doing because the very act of putting a church on sacred land disempowered the Indians from their spiritual connections to the Creator, their Spiritual Force and the Kachinas, the spirits of their ancestors.

As we shall see, it happened frequently and exists even to this day.

In the years that followed a second pueblo revolt was thwarted by the Spanish administration in 1696. The Pueblo Indians watched – and occasionally protested – as the new civilization arrived to dominate the high deserts. Albuquerque was founded and in the mid-1700s French trappers reached Santa Fe and began trading with the Spaniards. In 1821 Mexico declared independence from Spain and the famous Santa Fe Trail, an ancient passageway 800 miles in length, was developed for use by merchant-traders from Missouri. They brought manufactured goods to Santa Fe in exchange for furs, animal skins, turquoise and silver items.

In 1828 Coronado must have spun in his grave at the Church of Santo Domingo in Mexico City when gold was discovered in the Ortiz Mountains south of Santa Fe. Between then and 1965 over 2.25 million ounces of gold were mined in the area.

David E. Stuart in his extraordinary book *Anasazi America* says the descendants of Chaco Canyon have not only survived but in 1990 they numbered 55,330. This was according to the U.S. Bureau of the Census and at all reports their numbers continue to grow.

If one looks at the locations of you will see that the great majority of the Pueblos are in the region of the Rio Grande and the Sangre de Cristo Range with the Taos Pueblo in the north and the Isleta Pueblo a short distance south of Albuquerque. The area contains what the Tourism promoters call "The Enchanted Circle." This may sound a PR gimmick but as we shall see, through dowsing and the reading of earth energy, it is a powerful, magical healing circle with a system of beacons radiating far-reaching influences.

The Anasazi knew the power of these sacred energies. They were the First Wave to be and stay attracted. In modern times the mystical ways of the Pueblo Indians are under attack, not from warring nomadic tribes, not from drought and famine, not from catastrophic sickness, but from the very thing they have joined — evolution.

Every day thousands of Pueblo Indians, men and women venture out into the cities to work in offices, businesses, government departments and stores. They speak English and or Spanish for most of the day and when they return home to speak Tewa their tribal language they find their children have been talking English all day at school. Efforts to speak the old traditional languages are weakening and many elders fear the ancient languages are being lost.

So too are the shamans, the medicine men, the people who remember the old ways of prayers, singing and the rituals that connected them to the sipapu and the spirits of the ancestors. The presence of the churches on the pueblos create double loyalties and many Native Indians fear they are losing the old mystical ways.

The geospirals and perhaps the vortex that exists will save them. The question is how?

4

THEY CAME SEEKING UTOPIA?

Did the Spaniards fail to recognize the power of the Enchanted Circle because they were more materialistic? Or were they curbed from metaphysical and earth energy exploration by the fact that representatives of the Spanish Inquisition worked among them? Some people claim the second wave attracted by the powers of the Enchanted Circle started with the arrival in the closing stages of World War I of an east coast socialite named Mabel Dodge who would soon marry a Native Indian and become Mabel Dodge Luhan.

No, the second wave started with Christopher Houston Carson, otherwise known as Kit Carson, frontiersman, Indian fighter, trapper, Army scout and explorer of the west. His adventurous life and participation in a number of historical events brought him fame throughout North America and Europe. In his lifetime he was the hero of many dime novels and his name lives on in Kit Carson Electric Cooperative, many schools, Carson College and if you travel the highways you will wonder where the Carson National Forest starts and finishes. Covering 1.5 million acres it contains some of the finest mountain scenery in the southwest and stands frequently in the clouds between 6,000 and 13,161 feet. That is Wheeler Peak, the highest point in New Mexico.

Carson first visited Taos as a teenager and got a job with Matthew Kinkead who taught him the art of trapping. Consequently he came back to Taos with its Enchanted Circle many times and eventually settled in the growing community to raise his children. He died of an aneurysm in Fort Lyon Colorado and was buried next to his wife in the cemetery in the center of Taos. His headstone inscription reads: "Kit Carson / Died May 23, 1868 / Aged 59 Years."

One wonders why he called Taos his home because there were so many other potential places he discovered in his travels such as the Pacific Ocean which he claimed was the most beautiful water he had ever seen. But if the truth be known he too felt the tug, the powerful magnetism of the earth energy in the Taos region. The traveler will find Kit Carson's home just off the main street Paseo del Pueblo Norte on – yes, you have guessed it — Kit Carson Street. The National Park named after him is also a few paces along the Paseo.

Just along the street from the Carson house there is Morada Lane which really needs to be called Celebrity Row because everyone who was anyone in the Golden Age of entertainment and the arts traveled down this road to see Mabel and Tony.

HELLO MABEL

The Buffalo Bisons Baseball Club was preparing for its first season at Riverside Park in western New York State when Mabel Ganson was born into a wealthy family in February 1879. Through marriage and powerful connections she enhanced her wealth and became a prominent figure in the dizzy world of the arts and society both in New York City and Florence, Italy. Her days were filled with writers, artists, activists, pioneer filmmakers, musicians, in fact anyone whose work was innovative, experimental or unconventional, in other words on the cutting edge. A fabled hostess, she was the talk on both sides of the Atlantic.

Then suddenly in 1916 when the war in Europe cast a dismal gloom over America, Mabel Dodge packed her bags and headed for...where? Taos? New Mexico?

Friends and connections were stunned. "Why, I hear it's a one-horse town and the horse has bolted," a friend once quipped. Her seemingly madcap plan made front page news. Here was a vivacious thirty-seven year old wealthy influential woman heading for the wild deserts and mountains of New Mexico and few could understand why.

Maurice Sterne, the sculptor and artist and her third husband, recognized her disillusionment with Europe and the mind-shattering bloody reports from Flanders and suggested Mabel spend some time out west — California. Someone mentioned Taos, and with a growing curiosity, she stopped in the small, dusty, almost sleepy little town that had seen its last as a fur trading center.

In a short space of time — seven years — Mabel purchased a rustic three-bedroom adobe house that overlooked a Taos Pueblo sagebrush landscape and purple hazed mountains, divorced the sculptor and married a cool, dignified, philosophical man from Pueblo named Tony Luhan. Unmistakably Indian, he came with two long braids of black hair and wore a traditional Indian-weave blanket. There was something about the Native Indians that attracted and intrigued Mabel. They lived and manifested a certain mysticism upon which she talked and wrote but was never accurately able to define.

Still, she started to attract an impressive and almost non-stop parade of some of the world's greatest artists, writers, philosophers, composers, poets and freeloaders. Some came for a weekend while others came for longer periods such as months and some came for life.

One was Georgia O'Keeffe who was captured by the region's majestic landscapes, with its unusual mysterious chasms and wild, majestic rock formations. She was captivated by the vivid colors that changed as the day changed and the clarity of pure light so much so that it kept her magnetized for more than four decades. Originally a visitor to Mabel's place she made her home in Santa Fe and later in the desert town of Abiquiui plus a retreat at the nearby Ghost Ranch. The force that attracted her there enabled her to become an outstanding American artist and although she visited the Luhans frequently there was never a real understanding between the two women. Georgia O'Keefe crossed into Spirit in March 1986 at the grand old age of 98. Her ashes were scattered atop Pedernal Mountain in the heart of "O'Keefe Country." Stand on the shore of Abiquiui Lake and look south and you cannot miss the tabletop mesa.

One man who turned up and spent the winter of 1924 in Taos was the great Swiss psychiatrist and psycho-analyst, Carl Gustav Jung. In an interview with Chief Mountain Lake of the Taos Pueblo he endeavored to discover the true mysticism possessed by the Native Indians. He came no nearer than did Mabel in her efforts — and she was married to an Indian.

The parade that came to the little dusty town of Taos over the 46 years Mabel Dodge Luhan was in residence included photographer Ansel Adams, artist Salvador Dali and British novelist W. Somerset Maugham both of whom spent the war years working in the U.S. and visited Mabel. Dali brought his wife Gala, the former wife of Paul Eluard, the poet and founder of the Surrealist Movement. The Dalis also spent time with British poet Edward James who made a home in Taos as did the English artist John Young Hunter who painted a famous portrait of Mabel and

Pulitzer Prize winner Edna Ferber who wrote novels including *Show Boat, Cimarron* and *Giant* which were all made into successful movies.

Other visitors included Thomas Wolfe, Moira Shearer and the wealthy oil-heiress Millicent Rogers who stayed to create an impressive museum of Native Indian art and jewelry, contemporary paintings, weaving and pottery. Greta Garbo at the height of her career as a Hollywood star took time out to yield to the magnetism of Taos. The beautiful Swedish actress came on the arm of Mabel and Tony's friend Leopold Stokowski, then the popular conductor of the Philadelphia Symphony Orchestra.

The parade of worldly stars kept coming. Thornton Wilder, Willa Cather, Thomas Wolfe, Carl Sandburg, John Galsworthy and then there was Sinclair Lewis. The very prolific, radical-thinking Lewis and his wife made several visits to Taos and it was shortly after their visit that Sinclair took an interest in psychic phenomena and experimented with telepathy. His book entitled *Mental Radio* was published in 1930 and included accounts of his wife Mary's experiences and ability. It created upheavals among followers, most of whom saw him as a corporate and political muckraker and not a metaphysicist or spiritualist.

Taos energy created endless stories. One concerned two famous artists who were guests of Mabel and Tony. Arnold Rönnebeck met Louise Emerson in the electric energy of the Luhan camp in the summer of 1925 and they were married the following March at the All Angels Episcopal Church in Manhattan. Of course, Mabel and Tony Luhan attended, except that Tony entered in full formal Indian attire, ceremonial ribbons in his braids and wrapped in his traditional tribal blanket. Normally the spotlight at a wedding is on the bride but when a fully dressed Indian turns up in Manhattan... Well, as one can imagine it prompted lots of gossip and news coverage.

On a visit to Taos in 1933 Myron Brinig met Mabel who immediately took a liking to the novelist and invited him to stay with her. Brinig spent the summer in one of Mabel's guest houses with the modernist painter Cady Wells. He and Wells would live together as lovers for the rest of that year and most of the next. In 1936 while alone in San Francisco he wrote his best-seller *The Sisters* which was made into a hit movie starring Bette Davis and Errol Flynn. The movie was released in 1938 and with the money he made from that film Brinig returned to Taos and bought a house where he lived for the next 16 years soaking up the energy. He crossed into Spirit in 1991 aged 94 years.

"Like to like, the magnetic ones flew to the magnet. Impelled by a mysterious gravitation, the glowing spirits arrived every month every week, and added their luster to the lustrous Valley," Mabel wrote in a 1951 article published in the *New Mexico Quarterly*.

It was in the early 1920s that the controversial and self-exiled English writer D. H. Lawrence arrived with his wife Frieda, a distant relative of the "Red Baron" Manfred von Richthofen, and a young English painter Lady Dorothy Brett. "The Brett" as she was known, adored Lawrence and when they acquired a small ranch, Lady Brett lived in a one room cabin next door and typed the great author's manuscripts. Incidentally Dorothy Brett stayed in Taos for life and became one of its greatest artists and promoters.

But the air at "Los Gallos" as Mabel's place became known was always electric. Mabel well describes this energy in her book *Lorenzo in Taos* which contain her memoirs of Lawrence, published after his death in 1930.

If you think that Mabel's place radiated a "lazy days of summer sitting under the shade of a massive cottonwood sipping endless mint juleps" atmosphere you would be dead wrong. Everyone came reeking with energy and consequently there were frequent irrational, egotistical and dramatic scenes between the players. As we will relate later, the wife of a famous American poet gripped with jealousy tried to kill herself.

This is one of the problems of the geospiral and the vortex. While they generate beautiful inspiring energies and creative, even romantic thoughts, if your mind and body cannot receive them, you will be drawn to crazy and sometimes dangerous acts. It happens frequently in high society, Hollywood and corporate life. Unable to handle the creative and cosmic powers it may drive people to drugs, extra-marital affairs, spending sprees that end in bankruptcy, or simply making rash and unwise decisions.

Mabel adored and desperately sought an intimate relationship with Lawrence. This created severe pangs of jealousy in the minds of wife Frieda and Lady Brett. Husband Tony Luhan unable to stand the wild and electric energy would sneak off to the Taos pueblo to wait until the current upheaval subsided, but some say it was to spend time with his former wife.

Lawrence, aloof and possibly grinning inside his somber bearded face, wrote every day and seemed impervious to the whims and fancies of the women. Yet, they all frequently gathered for dinners at Los Gallos also known as The Big House, picnics in the foothills of the Sangre de Cristo Mountains that flanked Taos and the Lawrence Ranch, or they simply lounged on the terrace at Los Gallos. Nothing was ever quiet. The nearest thing to meditation was a quiet morning nursing a hangover. If you gather a pack of thoroughbred race horses together nothing is ever quiet and relaxing and this was Taos in the Mabel years.

Lawrence frequently felt the power that urged many to be in New Mexico and he rode it like a wild stallion. Several times he told Mabel "This is one of the magnetic centers of the earth."

In the scant two years he was in Taos he rewrote and published *Studies in Classic American Literature*, critical essays started in 1917. He then completed new fictional works including *The Plumed Serpent, St. Mawr, The Boy in the Bush, The Princess* and various short stories. In addition he found time to create some more writings on travel that became *Mornings in Mexico*. It was in the short story *The Woman Who Rode Away* that Lawrence seemed to embrace the mysticism and spiritual consciousness of the Native Indians – the force that attracts people to the Taos region, the Enchanted Circle. The story ends at a cave near Taos and in our search for the magnetism Betty Lou and I were ultimately drawn to that cave in the heart of the Sangre de Cristo Mountains.

MABEL RAISES HER ENERGY SIGHTS

Meanwhile Mabel rode the crest of the energy wave that attracted so many well educated men and women of cosmopolitan society to the dusty little town tucked away in the valley of the Rio Grande. Frustrated that she could not find the spirit awareness and higher consciousness that seemed to elude her, she expanded her horizons and zeroed in on Europe again and a radical philosopher named George Gurdjieff.

Gurdjieff was born about 1870 in Armenia and during his travels he spent some fifteen years among the Sufis, the mystics of Islam. The Sufis are the descendents of mysterious origin in India, the Aryans who in turn were also descended, as some claim, from the survivors of Atlantis.

In essence the Sufis teach a "reparation of the heart and turning it away from all else but God." Based on his learnings among the mystics

Gurdjieff announced that humankind is totally asleep and has no real consciousness otherwise it would not kill, conduct wars, maltreat other humans regardless of origins, abuse, enslave and perform barbaric acts as if it were their right and do it in the name of God. "Man is asleep," said Gurdjieff, "He has no real consciousness or will. He is not free; to him, everything happens. He can become conscious and find his true place."

Gurdjieff's teachings which were claimed to be original urged people to impartially observe themselves, their thinking and their habits and perform this exercise without judgment, opinion or comment. It is then that the truth becomes evident and people attain Now consciousness, which is total freedom. As Paul Brunton succinctly wrote in his famous *Notes* it is "the human ego must be crucified." Incidentally these teachings are the subject of my book *Cracking the Glass Darkly*.

But Gudjieff ardently believed in humankind. "Man's possibilities are very great," he wrote. "You cannot even conceive a shadow of what man is capable of attaining..."

Mabel desperately wanted Gurdjieff to leave his home base at the Prieuré des Basses Loges in Fontainebleau-Avon near the famous Château de Fontainebleau and come to Taos. To get him she needed an envoy and his name was Jean Toomer.

Toomer was an American poet and novelist whose publication in 1923 of *Cane*, a book part drama, part poetry, part fiction that powerfully evoked Black life in the southern states and brought him universal acclaim as the most gifted African American of his generation. Deprived of a paternal upbringing and uncomfortable with his black identity — he simply wanted to be known as an American — he searched for a new way of living and found it in the fall of 1923. He met Gurdjieff and immediately became enmeshed in the teachings.

Mabel first met Toomer in New York where he explained the basic teachings and the spiritual freedom that Gurdjieff's philosophy offered. It was not a religion, simply a different way of living, he said. This was late 1925. Mabel's high hopes that the great master would come to Taos were dashed when to her distain she heard Gurdjieff was in France slowly recovering from a near-fatal accident on the road between Paris and Fontainebleau.

Not to be outdone, Mabel gave Toomer $14,000 to build an institute for the Gurdjieff teachings in Taos. The writer came and spent the winter of 1925-26 discussing the project. By 1927 Mabel's passion for either the good looking Jean Toomer or the Gurdjieffian teachings had faded and although Toomer returned to Taos several times in the next few years, the Taos Center never got off the ground and Mabel, according to her writings, never got her money back. Although Toomer did break with Gurdjieff in 1935, he succumbed to the region's magnetism, rented a house in Taos and rode the prevailing energy that attracted and encouraged writers and artists.

Lawrence, fatally ill in Italy wrote to Mabel Dodge Luhan that he desperately wanted to return to Taos and New Mexico because as he said several times, it was the magnetism. He believed there were healing powers, restorative energies in Taos.

Mabel herself recognized the energy of the Enchanted Land. Once, a friend wondered how Mabel could spend so many years in a remote vllage in New Mexico. Mabel responded: "I have no news, nothing happens here but miracles." Her 1935 book *Winter in Taos* is listed among the 100 Best Books In New Mexico.

In 1925 the novelist Willa Cather and her companion and lover, Edith Lewis arrived in Santa Fe and found the idea for her next book, *Death*

Comes for the Archbishop. The novel is based on the life of Jean-Baptiste Lamy and partially chronicles the construction of the Cathedral Basilica of St. Francis of Assisi which stands at the center of old Santa Fe.

Mabel Dodge Luhan invited the couple to come to Taos, and it was there in the Pink House, an annexe of Los Gallos, that Cather started writing the book. Tony Luhan escorted Cather to places she wished to visit and Lewis claims that the writer in her book modeled the Indian, Eusabio, after Tony Luhan.

The Amercan poet, Robinson Jeffers and his wife Una took summer vacations at the home of Mabel and Tony where they mingled with other artists and intellectuals. The Robinson Jeffers Association reports that during their 1938 stay in Taos, Mabel Luhan encouraged a liaison between Jeffers and another guest. When Una discovered this it triggered the most infamous episode in their married life ending with Una's attempted suicide by gunshot. It happened in Mabel's bathroom and by a sheer fluke the attempt failed. Una recovered and after their return to Carmel the Jeffers' family life gradually returned to normal.

As we mentioned earlier, high earth energy is a very difficult commodity to understand. First, it is generally unpredictable. Second, it moves in waves and carries people either to success or rejection and sometimes to self-destruction. The energy of the Enchanted Land can be either warm, cherishing and inspiring, or it can make your life miserable and drive you out of town on the first bus. If you need physical or mental help it will heal you. If you respond negatively with fighting and challenge it will kill you psychologically or even physically.

In the first forty years of the 20th century, writers, artists, dancers, photographers, poets, journalists and hangers on all trooped into the Enchanted Land between Santa Fe, Chimayó, Truchas, Espanola, Abiquiui and Taos. Many bathed in the energy and the magnetism they thought they had created, little aware that it was the same energy from the depths of the Earth that had attracted the migrants from Chaco Canyon eight centuries before.

It would have been enlightening to have looked into the past lives of some of the emigrants who suddenly dropped what they were doing, and hustled off to the Enchanted Land in search of a Mecca, a new Jerusalem, salvation. In a short space of time it became a prestigious art colony led by Andrew Dasburg, Leon Gaspard and Nicholai Fechin.

The Russian born Fechin was another example of the healing powers of the region. He developed tuberculosis in the early 1920s, visited Taos in 1926, realized the healing values of earth energy and moved to the town in 1927 and stayed for six years becoming a catalyst in the great south western art movement. After many travels, he settled in Santa Monica, taught many students, and died in 1955 generally clear of the TB that had plagued his earlier years. Incidentally Andrew Dasburg died in Taos at the age of 92.

Leon Gaspard, another Russian émigré artist arrived in New Mexico in 1918. Badly injured in World War I aerial battles in France and spent two years in hospital before he arrived in Taos and painted the latillas in Mabel's Rainbow Room where she did much of her writing. Gaspard died in Taos at the age of 82.

The Enchanted Land with its epicenter somewhere between Santa Fe and Taos attracted countless numbers of artists. There is an excellent website www.taospainters.com which names many of them and displays their works.

Upon reflection I personally believe that D.H. Lawrence suffering from tuberculosis desperately wanted to return to Taos not because of the social life nor from finding a place to write (he did this wherever he traveled) but from the special force, the special healing power of the Earth energy. Had he succeeded in getting back he might have received healing and produced many more novels, poems and stories for the world and lived to perhaps 1975, which would have made him 90 years of age As it was he died in Vence, France on March 2, 1930 at the age of 44. His ashes are entombed in a concrete memorial near the ranch where he lived and wrote for a brief period, a few miles north of Taos.

Frieda Lawrence who lived at the Ranch, died on her birthday August 11th 1956 at the age of seventy-seven.

Mabel Dodge Luhan crossed into Spirit at the age of eighty-two on August 13th 1962 after a forty-six year reign in the Enchanted Land as a fabled hostess of the avante-garde in the arts and society. Her body was laid to rest in the Kit Carson Cemetery. Her husband, Tony Luhan, who had been swept along to fame by Mabel's activities died a year afterwards. His family buried him in the Indian graveyard that lies within the walls of the remains of the original church at Taos Pueblo.

Lady Dorothy Brett Brett who accompanied Lawrence to Taos in 1924 stayed on in the town until her death in 1977. Feeling the magnetism and the power, she created new art techniques to paint the Indians and their ceremonies and became one of the stalwarts of art in New Mexico. In 1933 she wrote the book *Lawrence and Brett*. Though she never married she did during her life have two grand affairs, one with Lawrence and one with Stokowski. Her life spanned 93 years.

Life was good in the dusty little town that had attracted a maelstrom of personalities, but things were changing in the neighborhood and the energies were calling to new people with new ideas.

5

HIPPIES, EASY RIDERS AND EARTHSHIPS

They felt the energy and calling of the Sangre de Cristo Mountains and the valley of the Rio Grande that had become the homeland for the descendants of Chaco Canyon and Bandelier. They soon learned that not all newcomers were welcome in the Enchanted Land.

In the 1960s a new light shone across the country. John F. Kennedy promised change and many Americans truly believed it was the dawning of a golden age. It just did not happen. The Cuban Missile Crisis occurred and a major war was narrowly averted. Racial rioting erupted in key cities. President Kennedy and his brother Senator Robert Kennedy were both assassinated. Martin Luther King led the historic March on Washington, then he too was assassinated. The Vietnam war came into living rooms via television and the masses marched and protested. It was a time for rebellion and the younger generation carried the banners.

In the late 1960s they called them "Flower Children" or simply "Hippies." The movement was radical and widespread. Rebellion against the restrictions of society became rampant. Some thinkers declared it was the savage and unexpected change to the Rock and Roll era of the late 1960s that energized radical change.

Hippies were known for their belief in ideas of peace, never ending parties with enormous supplies of psychedelic drugs, music and dance.

Free sex and love were openly available. The hippies believed that life is a gift to embrace and enjoy so they left home, attended such events as Woodstock and hiked the lanes and byways of America singing songs of love and unity, drinking beer and smoking pot, grass, mary jane otherwise know as marijuana.

They were clad in brightly colored loose clothing, tie-dyed garments, patchwork jeans, long and full skirts, vests, peasant blouses, much of it self-made as a jesture of defiance to big business. Flea markets and used-clothing stores became the hippie markets and the demand for their style of clothes triggered back-street stores that catered to their needs. Hippies frequently wore Native American jewelry, strings of long beads and rainbow colored head bands and scarves.

The west coast of Canada, the United States and Mexico were the targets. An estimated half a million flocked to the Pacific shores of North America from Long Beach in British Columbia down to the beaches of California and Mexico. Haight-Ashbury became a mecca but it filled to overflowing and the flower children asked: "Where now?" Then somebody mentioned a Utopia called Taos.

The local media described the coming as an invasion. The locals felt it was a moral attack that undermined the very roots of their Utopian goals. The hippies saw the valley as a modern-day Eden with great opportunities for gardens, vegetable farming and agricultural independence. Some claimed it was "voluntary primitivism" and they "felt the calling."

Many saw it as an image of America as it should be. They too had visions of Utopia that did not match the visions of the Taoseans. There were rumors that a hippie supporter planned to buy 100,000 acres of land in northern New Mexico and there was talk that Taos could be the "hippie capital" of America.

By 1969 estimates suggested the hippie population of Taos stood at 2,000. One can well imagine the reaction of the resident population which stood at a mere 3,500. That was 1.75 Taoseans to every hippie. It sent a sharp ripple through the Cosmic energy.

The "invaders" came on foot, wildly painted old buses and ancient cars and within a short time northern New Mexico, mainly in the the Rio Grande valley, was home to over 30 communes and the heavy aroma of burning marijuana filling the very essence of what was Taos — the streets, the shops, cafes and of course the Kit Carson National Park.

In 1970 while the hippie clans were in residence the DEA classified the marijuana as a Schedule I Drug citing the plant to have the highest drug abuse potential alongside LSD and heroin thereby terminating a 120 year use as a pharmaceutical commodity for various conditions including nausea and labor pains.

The Taos Chamber of Commerce charged that the presence of the hippies was a direct threat to the fragile economy. Directors were fearful that tourist numbers would decline.

Some affluent hippies were able to buy large parcels of land from local farmers and land owners, mainly Hispanics who had suffered a series of depressions since the 1930s. This triggered escalating real estate values and an ensuing bitterness among non-hispanics. In the mid-fifties the Taos Ski Valley took shape and downhill skiing became the "in" thing in the 1960s which brought in the après-ski crowd of happy sometimes rowdy drinkers and dancers. This triggered a real estate boom in select regions, notably areas adjacent to mountains such as Taos.

Change is one thing but the change the hippies brought was like the aliens coming from outer space. Many Taos businesses and stores displayed cards announcing that service would be refused to anyone considered a "health menace." There were signs such as "Keep America Beautiful: Take a Hippie to a Carwash." The situation rapidly deteriorated as the media reported violent clashes, hippie houses being shot up, sexual assaults on hippie women and several death threats. Several hippie vehicles were torched and some hippies reported being threatened by a lynch mob. Police meted out much harsher penalties to hippies than they did for locals.

In the summer of 1970 hippies put out warnings on the highways and calls were made to media on the west and east coast: "Taos is dead! This is a plea for help. Do not come. Stay away."

The peace and the visions of a Hippie Utopia were crushed overnight and so too was the vision of Utopia created by Mabel Dodge Luhan. Utopia was dead on the mortician's slab. This is one of the problems of Earth Energies. It can attract and give or it can attract and repel. It can also heal and make one feel good just living in its area of influence.

It is strange that the Hippie culture which promoted itself as back to the Earth and the natural life should have collapsed but as one observer once noted: "They were so busy protesting the establishment and making a statement they ignored the Earth and its Cosmic energies. If they had been aware, they would have stayed in the Enchanted Land."

One day Dennis Hopper, Jack Nicholson and Peter Fonda rode into town on their motor bikes and made the classic movie *Easy Rider*. Some say that was the start of the Enchanted Land attracting movie productions. Not so, Thomas Edison in 1898 visited the Isleta Pueblo near Albuquerque and made a short movie *Indian Day School* which can be viewed on Youtube.com. Hopper did bring a form of commercial cinema — and his own brand of protests to northern New Mexico.

Easy Rider came out in 1969 and Hopper used the late Mabel Dodge Luhan's Los Gallos to assemble and edit the film. His contribution to the

American film industry was extensive as actor, filmmaker, artist and photographer but wherever he worked he always returned to Taos even after death.

Aged 74 Dennis Hopper died in Venice, California where in his later years he had made his home and his body was returned to Taos. His funeral took place on June 3, 2010 at San Francisco de Asis Mission Church in Ranchos de Taos, New Mexico. He was buried in Jesus Nazareno Cemetery, Ranchos de Taos. The earth energies attract even in death.

One set of newcomers who felt the attraction of earth energy and moved in almost unnoticed during the 1960s were the creators of the Lama Foundation, Steve Durkee, Barbara Durkee and Jonathan Altman. Construction started on 109 acres for "a sustainable spiritual community and educational center dedicated to the awakening of human consciousness, spiritual practice with respect for all traditions, service, and stewardship of the land." Some observers noted it was almost as if Mabel was working in the Spirit World to get this project happening.

The Lama Foundation is 20 miles north of Taos in the foothills of the Sangre de Cristo Mountains and borders the Kit Carson National Forest to the north. The land and air itself feel special, imbued with a unique holy vibration that cannot help but nurture one's deepest places. Visitors from all over the world generally agree they have created beautiful and sacred natural buildings that may give one a-worldly Utopian feeling. From the original geodesic Dome to the sky-lighted kitchen and to the unique Hermitages and residences, the Lama Foundation has become a cutting edge school for natural building and permaculture practices. The whole community is completely off-grid generating electricity through photovoltaic cells or solar panels, using compost toilets, wood for heat, and water from an on-site spring. They also collect rain water. Water is heated in the main through a propane heater because the solar capacity is limited.

The Lama Foundation welcomes all spiritual traditions. Ram Dass collaborated with the Lama residents to create his seminal volume *Be Here Now* in 1970. The Sufi Saint Murshid Samuel Lewis chose Lama Foundation as his final resting place in 1971. There is a long list of other spiritual teachers who have taught at Lama including: Meher Baba, Stephen Levine, Jack Kornfield, Baba Hari Dass, Chogyam Trungpa Rinpoche, Father Thomas Keating, Rabbi Zalman Shachter-Shalomi, and Joshu Sasaki Roshi. Each summer, Lama continues to offer a diverse calendar of retreats and educational programs. Was this the vision Mabel possessed back in the 1920s? Whatever, the earth force continued to attract.

While the Lama Foundation was taking root north of Taos, another project was forming across the Rio Grande that would influence developments around the world. The prime mover and shaker was and is a fellow named Michael E. Reynolds.

A MAN WITH A VISION OF EARTHSHIP TAOS

Fresh out of architecture school at the University in Cincinatti in 1969, Michael Reynolds moved to Taos. During earlier vacations he had spent time in the area and "loved it." He had heard that the mountain of the Pueblo Indians was one of the power spots on the planet. Once in Taos he never wanted to leave. "Something happened to me here. I felt so at home that I think I must have stumbled onto my own energy," he writes in his book *A Coming of Wizards*.

He explains: "What I mean is, I found that particular state of mind which allows the oneness or wholeness of the universe to prevail over human dogma. I believe this state of mind is a key to the limitless energy of the universe."

Enthralled with pyramids he created a large perfectly scaled one on top of his house, and positioned his bed right at the King's Chamber. As he lay there, he became acutely conscious that he was sleeping in a "beautiful valley at the base of a sacred power mountain, in a land so akin to my essence of my own being that I felt like it ran in my body, through my veins and out again."

As an archictect and builder Reynolds began to reflect on what was happening to him. "The Earth became a sacred place that I wanted human life to embrace rather than exploit," he wrote. "I became focused on developing self-sufficient housing made from recycled materials using energy from the sun and wind."

It was in the early 1970s while in the pyramid that he began having "intense experiences, dreams, instances of automatic writing and outright visions." He stresses he was not on any drug, alcohol or other mind altering substance when one afternoon he was lying on his back in the pyramid and he experienced a spiritual visitation by four wizards.

"They clearly and vividly made me aware of a way of seeing and moving that grows in potential through use, with apparently infinite resonance," he says.

Adopting cautious consideration at first, he began to find similarities between their information, eastern mysticism and quantum physics, the ways of the Shaman, the nature of plants and animals and the processes of the planet itself. As he became more focused about the information, "I found myself on a journey to a world that reflects more than just the human condition." His thoughts, realizations and an upward change in consciousness are explained in his fascinating and inspiring book *A Coming of Wizards.*

In 1972 he built his first house from recycled materials. He utilized everyday discarded trash items like aluminum cans, plastic bottles and used tires. In place of conventional and energy-consuming recycling methods he used them as-is. He realized that any container and object, be it a soda bottle or an old tire, could be transformed into a powerful and durable insulation when filled with dirt. He calls this practice Earthship Biotecture and he has dedicated his life to it and authored at least five books on it.

If one heads out of Taos and crosses the great Rio Grande bridge which is 650 feet above the river and heads west a short distance on U.S. Route 64 the traveler will find Michael Reynold's work. It's called Earthship Taos.

Having been involved in metaphysics and dowsing for almost as long as Reynolds has been working on Earthship and still possessing conventional limitations, the sight on Route 64 is breathtaking because it is out of this world. It feels as if one has been dropped onto some lunar landscape, but there is an overwhelming energy which says "This is home. Stay awhile."

The reception center is an Earthship that is alive and well. Displays are illuminated by a 24-volt power system fed by solar panels. Attendants work on computers, a verandah is the home of various plants, and in the garden flanking the place we spotted gardeners at work. Betty Lou and I stood there gazing across the the undulating, sun-bleached desert sprinkled with sagebrush that dances in the afternoon breeze. A yellow sandy, unpaved roadway leads off into the distance. A sign announces "Greater World Earthship Community — Residents Only."

We wondered how many Earthship homes were out there.

"Seventy," replies an attendant.

We ask if we can see Mr. Reynolds.

"Oh, he's away in West Africa, the Republic of Sierra Leone," she says. "They have an Earthship project being built there."

Apparently the Earthship Projects, a new way of living on the planet, the brainchild of Michael Reynolds in Taos over forty years ago, is alive and well. His battle with authorities is out of the realm of this book. Suffice to say he is one man who came to stay in Taos because he felt the energy, cosmic energy which gave him a vision and an edge. Incidentally, his book that we mentioned above is based on his journals and is a gem for students with visions who wish to understand physical achievement along with higher consciousness.

One note of caution: If you are considering making an Earthship your home, first get rid of all your preconceived ideas and fantasies and visit one with a completely open mind, because it is a new way of living. Oh yes, you can also rent an Earthship.

DOWSING THE EARTHSHIP

We discovered a geospiral in the most unexpected place — the store at the Information Center just off U.S. Route 64. It was radiating energy over most of the arrival center. The dowsing rods indicated there were several more "out there" among the Earthship Community which means it should be a very healthy place to hang hats and have children. Perhaps one day someone with dowsing abilities will conduct an Earthship survey.

We then asked the rods to show us the next step in our search for the power and the solitary search rod swung round to the Sangre de Cristo Mountains simmering in the purple afternoon haze. It was the second time the rods had pointed to the mountains. The question now was where — specifically?

6

FLAGELLATION AND A PAPAL MEDALLION

The first time we were returning from a visit to Questa storm clouds were massing in the Rio Grande Valley. As we drove towards Taos on Route NM522 we glanced towards the foothills of the Sangre de Cristo Range and a beautiful rainbow started forming in one of the valleys.

A lover of rainbows I stopped the car immediately, seized my camera and standing on the roadside took several shots of the forming rainbow. As I looked, it seemed to stop developing and simply froze creating a shimmering purple vision over the foothills. Then just as it had suddenly appeared, it vanished. People might think it strange but the rainbow incident occurred thirty seconds after I poked my head from the moving car window and called to God to "show us a sign." But that is the way we sometimes talk to the Cosmos.

We decided that was the region we must explore. The village snuggled in the foothills is Arroyo Seco, a quaint old world community just seven miles from Taos. It boasts one main street lined with small specialty shops, an excellent casual eating place named the "Taos Cow" and various services. Many of these shops exhibit work by local artists and crafts people, in fact the day we arrived there an artist with a wide brimmed sun hat, a smock, an easel and canvas was creating a work of art right on the side of the road. For fleeting moment I thought it was 1890 and Van Gogh was standing in the street of Auvers-sur-Oise, France.

Arroyo Seco is a Spanish term meaning "dry brook" or "dry stream." For two centuries it has attracted settlers and latterly celebrities in the way of authors, movie stars, and even hippies who have chosen to hide in mountainside homes cloaked by forests.

It rests in a valley between Taos Mountain, the domain of the Taos Pueblo Indians, and the sacred mountain of El Salto and is drenched in legends.

The way the locals tell it is two early settlers, the brothers Cristóbal and José Gregorio Martinez set off to work in the fields but because of reports of marauding Indians, they warned their children to stay close to home.

A short while later while the children played a shadow flickered in the sun Two figures approached. Startled, the children jumped up and a man's voice said "Fear not." The two newcomers were an elderly man with a long white beard and a young man who appeared to be his son. They explained they lived further down the valley and if the children followed the stream they would find them.

Naturally, the children asked why the two men were not afraid to be so far from home because of marauding Indians.

"We have a bird. The bird warns us whenever danger is near," replied the young man. The children went on playing then turning around they noticed the two men had suddenly disappeared.

That night they told their parents. Everyone became alarmed. The next day the two families set out to warn the two men about the danger of nomadic Indians. As they followed the stream a white dove appeared and seemed to lead them by hopping from branch to branch of trees lining the way. Finally, the bird settled on a particular stone for a few moments then flew up into a tree. Now brimming with curiosity the Martinez families lifted the stone and found a bulto or a carved ikon underneath.

The astonished children pointed to the portrayed figures. "Look, there's the old man with the white beard and his son standing beside him!" they cried. "And there is the bird!"

To the early settlers it was the Trinity — God the Father, his Son Jesus and the Holy Spirit in the form of a dove. It was at that point that the families knelt and prayed and dedicated the valley to the Holy Trinity.

When they built the church in 1834 it was named "La SantissimaTrinidad." Originally it had a flat roof and a dirt floor. No one seems to know who picked the site of the church, but one thing is for sure that person knew and understood Earth energies. Because right in front of the altar, centered on the church axis, there is a powerful geospiral that stretches way outside the walls of the old church. There is also a leyline coming through the village and passing along the church axis.

Over the years, modifications and improvements were made to the church and it served the growing community well until the 1960s when the building was deemed too small and a new building was constructed and named the Holy Trinity Church. It was positioned about 100 yards away at a right angle to the old church.

The original church building became a community center until its frail condition led to its closure in the late 1970s. In the 1990s an intense restoration effort started and strangely, another peculiar event occurred right in the center of the geospiral.

It involved a Pope and an Archbishop both long since dead. It happened this way.

A French priest, Jean Baptiste Lamy, who had studied and been ordained at Montferrand in France answered the call in 1839 for missionaries to America. First he served in Ohio and Kentucky and to his surprise was appointed Bishop of the newly created Vicariate of New Mexico on July 23,1850. He arrived in Santa Fe in the summer of 1851. Lamy was a tough disciplinarian. He pushed for the creation of new parishes, churches and schools. He ended the marriage of priests and with an iron rule suppressed religious brotherhood societies.

One such society was the Los Hermanos Penitentes, a group of people who atone for their sins by practicing penances which consist principally of flagellation, carrying heavy crosses, binding the body to a cross, and tying the limbs to hinder the circulation of the blood. The Catholic Encyclopedia gives many details on these societies and lists Colorado and New Mexico as main centers and lists Taos with 300 members.

Bishop Lamy discovered to his horror that the actual cornerstone of the Penitentes was to be found in Arroyo Seco. During his ad limina visit to Rome, Lamy reported to Pope Pius IX and to Cardinal Alessandro Barnabo, a dictatorial figure on congregational affairs, that a renegade group of Penitentes fanatics existed in Taos and Arroyo Seco and considered themselves the Church of New Mexico.

The Pope put it bluntly to Bishop Lamy. Get rid of them!

The Bishop returned with a gold plated bronze papal medallion featuring Pope Pius IX to be presented to Father Antonio José Martinez and the congregation of the La Santisima Trinidad Church at Arroyo Seco.

The Bishop asked the Father if he knew who was heading the Penitentes.

Father Martinez replied. "It is I. I am the leader of the Penitentes."

At that point, Bishop Lamy informed the Father that a papal order had been issued to terminate the Penitentes. To reinforce the order, the Bishop presented Father Martinez with the gold papal medallion.

Martinez exploded with anger and threw the medallion to the ground. It was promptly buried face down in the earthen floor of the church and forgotten.

Did the angry Father ever realize that where he had buried the papal medallion it rested within inches of the center of a very active geospiral? It's unlikely that he did simply because in the Laws of Metaphysics, dedicated fanatics in any modality usually do not possess psychic or dowsing sensitivities.

In 1915 the earthen floor of the church was covered over with wood as the building was upgraded and then in the 1970s the old church closed and replaced by the new Holy Trinity church across the way.

In the 1980s there were various plans discussed on renovating the old church and restoration was eventually carried out. As it did a strange event occurred in the old building.

It involved a tall and erect gentleman named Manuel Medina who proudly informed us he was eighty-two years old and custodian of the old church. He added proudly: "I speak Castillian Spanish from the old country." Apparently he is a direct descendant of the original Spanish settlers in the 17th century.

In 1987 while checking the old church foundations in preparation for restoration, he was working in the earth under the apse when to his utter surprise he found a gold-plated copper medallion some eight inches across. It was the papal medallion issued by Pope Pius IX, carried by Bishop Lamy and presented to Father Martinez.

Mr. Medina pointed to the medallion now encased in a cedar-lined box crafted by a local parishioner. It is mounted on the east wall of the church sacristy and appears as bright and shiny as the day it started its journey from Rome in the 1850s.

If the angry Father Martinez the head of the Penitentes had buried it anywhere else except the church which is protected by a sacred spiral of Earth energy, it may not have survived one and a half centuries in the mud.

The area of influence of the geospiral at the old Arroyo Seco church is about 75 yards and anyone sitting in the church for even a few minutes is bound to feel the healing energy.

There is a private residence close to the altar end of the old church and while we were standing outside I mentioned to Betty Lou that the people who lived there would certainly be healthy. Just then a young woman came from the home and opened her car door.

"Hello, is your family healthy living in that house?" I queried.

"Oh, yes, we are all very healthy. It's always very peaceful and when we are away, we cannot wait to get back home." She smiled and said her name was Caitlin.

We informed her of the beneficial geospiral energy. "Oh, I always thought because the mass is said there once a week that that was responsible," she said with another smile. "Now we know something else. Thank you."

We dowsed the whole area and failed to find any other geospirals either in or around the new church. However, we did find a triple hairline leyline coming down out of the Sangre de Cristo Mountains, flowing just a few inches to the north of the new church axis then across the yard where in some bushes it performs a sharp 90-degree left turn and runs through the old church axis, cutting through the geospiral and out into the village. It crosses the main street west of the Taos Cow Restaurant and heads across the fields towards the Taos Pueblo.

According to the leyline there was an option of two directions. One was to follow the leyline to the Taos Pueblo, the other was to follow the leyline into the mountains. We chose the mountains.

7

THE CAVE THAT INSPIRED
D.H. LAWRENCE

The dowsing rods pointed to it. A half formed rainbow had indicated a valley where we should look and that led us to an unusual mountain in the Sangre de Cristo Range called Lucero Peak, a massive rock form towering 10,780 feet.

The steep sides of the mountain are blanketed by cedars and firs and on the October day in 2011when Betty Lou and I laboriously climbed the ragged forest trail, a light blanket of snow had recently heralded the coming of an early winter. The mountain forms a foothill west of Wheeler Peak, the tallest mountain in New Mexico. Lucero resembles a sleeping bear covered by a thick round blanket of trees with a tiny but lively creek making a silvery hairline down its back.

Some fifteen hundred feet below the peak there is a cave mostly hidden by trees, bushes and thick dense undergrowth. The trail to and from the cave is flanked by a profusion of young aspens, their trembling leaves a brilliant yellow in the fall light and the route is littered with fallen trees and and branches. Directly above the cave there is a small gully and a silvery stream struggles bravely over the rocky rim and flutters easily down perhaps sixty feet to a shallow pool beside the cavern. They say that during the spring run-off or after a summer storm the stream becomes a raging torrent. Today it was a fluttering creek trying desperately to stay alive.

It is no easy task to get to the cave. First of all one has to buy a ticket from the land owners the El Salto Association. This is a permit to enter their property which includes part of Lucero mountain. Then one drives several miles along a tortuous dusty unpaved track that crosses various ridges and passes several mysterious estates with iron or steel gates and high fences. No names, no numbers, just notices declaring the obvious "Private Property. No Trespassing." A couple of movie people are supposed to spend time here but perhaps that's just a rumor.

When the car could no longer sensibly tolerate the rocky terrain, we walked along the track, passed through a gate and made our way among bushes and fallen branches, forever climbing upward, frequently stopping to regain one's breath. We estimated that we must be at the 9,000 foot level because every few yards we had to stop because our lungs were protesting and calling for air. Strangely in our enthusiasm to reach the cave we had left the oxygen cans along with water bottles back in the car. Even stranger we did this once before when we visited the Kelly Ghost Mine near Socorro. Age and enthusiasm overcome one's ability to remember lessons. Cameras and dowsing rods seem to take preference over life sustaining oxygen and water. So we stopped every few yards to let our lungs adjust.

We had to climb over a couple of fallen trees before the cave suddenly appeared. At first sight it looks dark, deep and vaguely monstrous but as one stands in the gaping mouth you realize it is harmless, in fact when the sun shines in the afternoon it is quite pleasant and a great place to have a picnic.

Picnic? Let us roll back the clock.

Almost ninety years before we visited here four horses made their way along the ill-kept trail. They carried four people all making their mark in history.

Mabel Dodge Luhan, her husband Tony Luhan, D.H. Lawrence also known as Lorenzo to Mabel, and Frieda otherwise known as Mrs. Lawrence.

The four explored the cavern that stands like a dark gaping hole in the side of the mountain. They peered into the tunnels and smaller caves that lead off the main cavern. The gaping hole in the mountain is so big that several full-sized buses could be parked easily side by side inside. Afterwards while sitting on rounded bolders flanking the stream they enjoyed a picnic.

The energy emanating from the cave captivated Lawrence's imagination because soon after he wrote a short story entitled "The Woman Who Rode Away." The tale concludes with a cave which he describes as "a dark socket, bored a cavity, an orifice, half way up the crag." That's exactly how the cave on Lucero Peak appears.

The story tells of a woman tired of conventional married life who takes a horse and rides off into the wilds and joins a band of Indians who happen to own a sacred cave.

As some alert critics point out in some ways the story reflects the situation of Mabel Dodge Luhan who rejected the heady world of arts and society in New York and Florence, Italy and a husband and sought a Utopian future with a Native Indian.

The cavern buried in the belly of Lucero Peak high above the village of Arroyo Seco is considered sacred by the Indians at nearby Taos Pueblo but today no one seems to know if they make use of the mystical earth energies that exist in the cave. They call it sacred but for what reason and purpose we had no idea at that time.

The cave is not all that close to their own Taos Mountain and the Taos Pubelo. Several Indians to whom I asked the question failed to offer an explanation other than to say "It's a sacred place." One Indian shook his head and said "It's not good."

This is strange because right in the center of the old cavern is a geo-spiral, quiet, powerful, its rings spreading outward and upward so that wherever you are in the cave, you are under its Area of Influence.

If one spends some time relaxing quietly inside the cavern you can feel the energy. It is distinct and all powerful. It comes over like an invisible presence. Not only that, it produces pleasant lucid dreams for several days afterwards.

In the center of the cave among the dust there is a special spot where if one stands still you can feel the earth energies emanating from deep below. One can imagine that if a person who was completely unaware stood inside the cave for just a few minutes, their imagination would start to kick in with all sorts of ideas, not necessarily positive. But that is a human frailty and a condition created by the "monsters under the bed" suggestion in childhood and a list of scary movies as one gets older.

Geospirals produce a beautiful and powerful healing aura. Now, if one goes to seek healing or rejuvenation you will succeed and be rewarded. However, if your mind is negative and skeptical the geospiral will not work even if you are truly sick, because your own mind is blocking it. These things I sensed simply by standing on geospirals.

Carrying my dowsing rods I walked back and forth and quickly ascer-tained the existence of a set of rings forming the geospiral. A small rock the size of a football poking up from the ground marks the geospiral in the center of the cave. While I took photographs and later shot some video material I sensed I was being followed so I turned sharply. Of course, there was no one there. At least in the physical. It was certainly not Betty Lou because I could see her down the slope outside the cave taking photographs of the small waterfall and the pool.

"You have questions?" The voice was soft and easy as if cushioned by felt.

"Do you come with love and light?"

The entity laughed. "You still have to ask the question like a student?"

"Protection," I said.

"You are no different from the others. Even my people carry their fears in their heads?"

"They told me at the Pueblo that while it is a sacred place it is also dangerous."

Suddenly, the spirit manifested into the physical and an aged leathery face burned by the hot desert sun and heavy with wisdom swung in front of me. "They have forgotten. They say they live by the old ways and they talk about the sky and the sun and the moon. They talk about the earth and the trees and the grass and how things are growing well this year but they do not know how to communicate." His dark eyes resembled pools in a dark lake. "My brothers and sisters have forgotten the old ways. Their eyes have become clouded. They have become influenced by the white people."

"Can you tell me about that?"

"Better. I will show you." His hand reached out and touched my face. "When you meditate I will come to you and I will explain how it is."

"When?"

"I will come."

"What is your name?"

"They call me Running Bear."

"An interesting name."

"It is of no importance. Your woman waits. I will come."

For hours afterwards as we roamed the little shops in Arroyo Seco, sipped hot chocolate at the Taos Cow and then drove back to the town, I could still feel the hand of the spirit on my face. I wondered what he would come to tell me.

PHOTOGRAPHS ALONG THE WAY
BY THE AUTHOR

Credit: All photographs in this section by the author: Robert Egby

WOODHENGE AT CAHOKIA, ILLINOIS. A circle of posts used to make astronomical sightings, west of the famous Monk's Mound. For the ancient Cahokians placement of posts marked solstices and equinoxes. As predicted by British Dowser Dennis Wheatley we found the first geospiral here on our journey. (Details Ch-2)

THE BIG KIVA at the Bandelier National Monument is set in the rugged cliffs and canyons of the Pajarito Plateau. Here we found a strong geospiral with an area of influence stretching beyond the walls. (Details Ch-3)

MABEL'S CASTLE in Taos. This was the tower where Mabel Dodge Luhan and her husband Tony Luhan lived. Mabel wrote all her books here where she envisioned a utopia far from the madding crowd. (Details Ch-4)

WALK OF THE FAMOUS. The entrance to Mabel and Tony's place. Stars such as Carl Gustav Jung, D.H. Lawrence, Georgia O'Keefe, Leopold Stokowski, and Greta Garbo were among the long list of personalities that walked this cobbled entrance. (Details Ch-4)

EASY RIDER. Remember the 1969 American road movie with Peter Fonda, Dennis Hopper, Jack Nicholson and Terry Southern and directed by Dennis Hopper? Sections were filmed on this main street in Taos. The bikers still come more than four decades later... (Details Ch-5)

THE EARTHSHIP AT TAOS. You will find it in the sweeping desert landscape west of Taos across the Rio Grande Gorge Bridge. It's what is known as radically sustainable buildings made with recycled materials. This is the creation of Michael Reynolds who now has projects around the world and he still calls Taos his base and home. (Details Ch-5)

A SIGN OVER THE MOUNTAINS appeared quite suddenly and in a few seconds was gone. We asked the Universe for a sign as to where we should search for geospirals. The sudden phenomenon appeared over Arroyo Seco and the Sacred Cave in the mountains. (Details Ch-6)

THE OLD CHURCH AT ARROYO SECO. The simple but beautiful place is packed with legends and mysteries. Yes, it is built upon a powerful geospiral positioned right in front of the altar that spreads positive healing energy to a nearby home. (Details Ch-6)

A PAPAL MEDALLION AT ARROYO SECO. This is the Papal Medallion given to the community by Pope Pius IX. It rested in the mud beneath the church floor for 140 years before being found over the geospiral – in perfect condition! (Details Ch-6)

THE SACRED CAVE. This cavern hidden in the hills behind Arroyo Seco gave author D.H. Lawrence the ending for his short story "The Woman Who Rode Away." Earlier it gave service as a healing center following the U.S. Army attack on the Taos Pueblo. There is a powerful healing geospiral in the cave. Betty Lou is pictured outside. (Details Ch-7)

THE FULLER LODGE AT LOS ALAMOS. Built in 1928 it became the living center for boys at the famous Ranch School until 1942 when it was acquired for the Manhattan Project team designing the atomic bomb. The building still serves the arts and creative community today and holds one of three geospirals in the community. (Details Ch-8)

THE FAMOUS SPIRAL STAIRCASE is to be found in the Loretto Chapel in Santa Fe. Each year thousands of people flock to see this miraculous creation. We wondered how many feel the energy of the geospiral radiating from the point where we took this picture. Many years before it had been an Indian Pueblo, likely a kiva site.(Details Ch-10)

SAINT FRANCIS CATHEDRAL designed by French architects and built by Italian stonemasons for Archbishop Lamy occupies the center of Santa Fe. It is on several leylines and contains one geospiral. (Details Ch-10)

THE INTERIOR OF THE CATHEDRAL shows its Gothic and Romanesque features. Did French architect Antoine Mouly know that the axis of the Cathedral was being built on a triple-haired leyline? (Details Ch-10)

CHAPEL OF THE BLESSED SACRAMENT flanks the main Cathedral and it contains a powerful healing geospiral which is directly in front of the altar. Is it a coincidence that Christian church designers knew of the ancient energies or did they simply follow the Indians? (Details Ch-10)

TUCKED AWAY IN THE FOOTHILLS of the Sangre de Cristo Mountains is the Sanctuario de Chimayó. Popularly known as the Lourdes of America its healing power draws thousands of pilgrims and visitors from across the country and the world. A triple-haired leyline flows close to the main axis.(Details Ch-11)

THE LEYLINE FLOWS from the church, touches the great tree and passes through the center of a newly built outdoor chapel. Both the church and the chapel contain healing geospirals and the seats are positioned on the energy rings. This is the place where they call the earth Holy Dirt.(Details Ch-11)

THE THOUSAND-YEAR-OLD TAOS PUBELO. Ansel Adams photographed it and Carl Gustav Jung came here to interview the Chief on his spirituality and mysticism. In olden times it was a hotbed of revolt. (Details Ch-12)

A CEREMONIAL POLE stands at the center of the Taos Pueblo plaza which is also the exact spot of a powerful geospiral. It is one of several in the Pueblo. The stream in the foreground provides the community with water from the sacred Blue Lake or Ba Whyea as it is known. (Details Ch-12)

A MONUMENT TO A BATTLE is the last standing remains of the original church at Taos Pueblo. It's also the home of a positive geospiral. History in a nutshell: The Indians assassinated at Taos the Territorial Governor Charles Bent in January 1847. The U.S. Army using artillery blasted the church where Indians had sought refuge... It was the last violent uprising by Taos Puebloeans. The battle for Ba Whyea in the 20th century was carried out in the halls of Washington. (Details Ch-12)

8

OUT OF BODY EXPERIENCES

To be honest I do not know whether Running Bear came to see me or I re-visited the Lawrence Cave but whatever it was it manifested as a strange experience.

Two days later just after 2:00 a.m. I was awake in our rented condo at Sonterra in Taos. A quick visit to the toilet ended with a return to bed and as my eyes closed I thought I would meditate in my usual way by relishing the quiet and solitude of the Here and Now. It is an excellent way of returning to a deep healthy sleep.

Suddenly a presence was there in the room. I felt my body being tugged but it was not my physical body but the astral body. Ever since my days of learning with British medium Patrick Young in Vancouver I had been aware of a phenomenon called Astral Projection. It is a duplication of one's physical body except it constitutes fine almost invisible energy. Most people unconsciously astrally project their bodies at night.

The astral body, devoid of physical encumbrances, moves both through the physical and spirit worlds to experience relationships, learnings, and sometimes provide assistance to people in dire need. Sometimes the memories of these experiences linger as dreams. "I felt as if I was flying," someone may remark or "I was in some remote country with some people giving them water."

There are also many people who deliberately practice and accomplish astral projection. This is not a new phenomenon. It's mentioned in Ecclesiastes 12:6 as the silver cord — that's the link between the physical and the astral bodies. Back in 1971 Robert Monroe triggered a modern popularity with his classic book *Journeys Out of the Body*.

There was no time to think. In a fraction of a second I was back in the cave except it was now well lit with oil lamps and candles. Blue-green smoke filled the upper reaches of the cave. Was this the same cave Betty Lou and I had visited and photographed earlier. There was something drastically different.

"You came." The voice was Running Bear except I could not see him.

"I'm in my bed meditating at two o'clock in the morning."

"Look at your bare feet."

My feet were there on the earth. It felt strange.

"Do not be concerned," said the Indian. "Your Inner Being – as you say your Astral Body – is simply away for while."

"Did you do this? I mean pull me out of my body?"

Suddenly I spotted the spirit body of Running Bear. He was shaking his head. "If you stop asking how things occur and simply learn from what is happening you will progress much more easily. You will notice that your people spend more time trying to figure out in their minds how things happen than actually learning from what they are seeing or feeling."

Somewhere in my mind, I agreed with his comment.

"Sit down," he commanded and immediately two small boulders appeared and we sat down.

"How did you do that?"

114

"You're still in the how mind. I did it with my consciousness. Accept it," he said easily, then quite casually asked: "May I read your mind?"

"I'm sure you can quite easily."

Running Bear paused. "You wish to hear of the end of the Chaco people," he said. "But first I need to reveal to you the mindset of the ancestors. When you hear of Native Indians it is mostly in ways of violence, anger and death. Even before the coming of the Europeans, these negative feelings existed. Tribes fought tribes, raided each other for slaves and new blood. The Anasazi as your people called them were different. They built a large community of farmers, traders and thought-thinkers and never considered raiding other tribes for anything."

"Thought-thinkers?"

Running bear gazed into the light of the oil lamp as if reminiscing. "Thought-thinkers were the philosophers, you might call them priests but they were in touch with the higher consciousness of the stars and the spirit-messengers of the stars. The spirits helped the thought-thinkers understand the ways of the great spirits, and that is why the great houses were built in alignment with the sun and the worlds out there."

The old man turned and stared at me. "That is why the Anasazi were different," he said slowly, "because they remembered their beginnings, their roots, their seeds, their origin in the lands far away and were fully aware of the futility of war. It was the thought-thinkers who conducted community discussions in the kivas and shared the knowledge that came from the stars." There was a pause and then he shrugged. "You have heard it before. All knowledge is eternal and is available to mental sympathy."

"The shamans, the medicine men, where did they come in?"

"Healing was a major responsibility," he said. "He was also responsible for protecting his people in many ways such as guarding against bad weather, poor harvest, loss of flocks, or almost any catastrophe and all spiritual ceremonies were under his charge."

"They worked with spirits?"

"Naturally. They were the communicators, the messengers, the facilitators whose work was to bring the spirits of the ancestors into the kivas."

"The sipapu? The channel to the Underworld. Is that where the spirits of the ancestors come from?"

"That is the traditional thought. Sometimes it is easier to to talk to the families with simple ideas that are easy to believe. Your teacher, the man they called Jesus, he spoke of his Father in Heaven but that was for the desert people to easily understand. We bury the bodies in the earth it is only natural for people to believe the ancestors are in the earth too."

His hand reached out and touched my arm. "You listen and speak with the spirits of the ancestors. Do they come from the underworld?"

"They come from the Spirit World."

"And where is that, Robert? Where is that?"

"Spirit is energy except that it is on a different vibration not easily seen by our physical bodies, but if one meditates and tunes in to higher consciousness, one can communicate with spirits," I explained. "This is done through people called mediums."

"The shaman is the medium for Native Indians," added Running Bear quickly. "The earth energy from the sipapu makes it easy for the shaman to bring in the spirits of the ancestors."

"From the underworld?" Instinctively, I sensed his answer.

"The Spirit World," he said. "It is everywhere. When your Chinese healer took you on an astral body excursion it was beyond this world, this universe. It was a different world entirely. It is foolish to consider the Spirit

World similar to your world and the Universe. It is much more beautiful and the pains of materialism, power and money no longer exist..."

"And the ego." I put in.

"Ah! Yes and that creature they call the ego. The curse of human-kind."

"The Anasazi," I started to ask, "from what you suggest, I feel they did not have the curse of the ego. Is that true?"

Running Bear ran his hands over the oil lamp as if seeking warmth. Finally, he turned and looked, his dark brown eyes seeming to pierce my consciousness. "Ah, yes, in spite of the efforts of the teachers the thought-thinkers, the ego came into the lives of my brothers. But that is for another time."

In a flash I was back in bed and suffering an overwhelming feeling of tiredness, slipped off into a deep healthy sleep.

THE DOWNFALL OF THE CHACO EMPIRE

It happened again the next night, just after 2:00 a.m. It was dark of course, yet in a moment everything was brilliant sunshine and everything around was desert, a vast arid and remote desert. Everything was calm, still as if frozen in time like a photograph. There was only one thing wrong – I was moving into the picture at a rapid rate. Then the sensation stopped and I recognized the ancient ruins of Chaco Canyon and the Great House at Pueblo Bonito.

Running Bear was seated on a rock. "Cast your eyes on the land," he commanded with a wave of his right hand. "It was not always like this. Once upon a time there were forests of tall trees, pastures of grasslands, rivers and streams and the animals roamed in freedom. Once upon a time the rains came frequently and the water maintained the cycles of life and it was good for the tribes who came."

"The Anasazi?"

The Indian nodded. "If you wish to call them that. They were also known by other tribes as the 'ancient ones' and the Navajo people knew them as 'enemy ancestors,' but they were really people of the sun.

"Because they worshiped the sun?"

"No, because they came from beyond the sun," Running Bear replied with an air of simplicity as if the statement was something I should have known. "They were an interesting people. They were unlike other tribes. While they had hunters for gathering meat and hides they had no warriors for war. If you tried to attack and kill an Anasazi he would protect himself and his family by passive action but in the end he would accept death quietly because he knew he would return to the land beyond the sun."

"That must have presented a strange face to his attackers."

"Of course. Many failed to understand the ways of the Anasazi and eventually refused to attack and left the people of the sun in peace."

Running Bear stood up and came towards me. "The question of why Chaco Canyon failed is uppermost in your mind," he said. It was not a question but a statement of fact.

"Do you often read people's minds?"

The old Indian shook his head. "Sometimes it is better to sit by a stagnant ditch," he said with a shrug.

"My senses tell me the problem with Chaco was that it grew too big," I suggested.

"That is a partial truth, Robert," said Running Bear. "Size is totally acceptable provided you have the environment to support it. The Chacoans failed to maintain the forests, the trees they used and their world started to crumble. It could not tolerate a prolonged drought. Without trees and plants the rains failed to come. As your stone people, the archeologists indicate there were many years and seasons when the rains failed to come. The field harvests of corn, chipalote, beans and squash were poor and insufficient to sustain the growing population. The hunters returned with little but rabbits and turkeys because the big animals had died or drifted away in search of water. It was the prolonged droughts that tore apart the very fabric of the Chacoan people."

"So people simply got up and left for greener pastures," I said.

"Think slowly," commanded the Indian. "The Chaco people had spent many years creating their dwellings, long houses and farms and the suggestion of moving away to new lands and rebuilding pueblos was not received very well. There were other developments."

"Sickness?"

Running Bear nodded. "Disease came in various pueblos at various times. Anemia became rampant. Mothers were lucky if babies lived out the year. Half of all newborns died and some mothers weak from starvation and malnutrition died with them. The spirit of the people became angry. They blamed the elders, they blamed the shamans for losing touch with the Great Spirits of the Earth and Sky. Their prayers went unanswered so prayer-sticks were broken. A passive peace-loving people became angry and where there is prolonged anger violence erupts. Several shaman and elders were killed. Some elders in different pueblos fled. They were difficult and turbulent times."

As Running Bear continued to speak a vision, a picture came between us, like a movie screen being suspended in space. "The agony of Chaco stayed for many years," he said as a picture of the sun-drenched adobe houses came into view. "There were other dangers, this time from outside. Other tribes who were suffering similar fates sent bands of warriors to search for food in deserted pueblos and forage among tribes that had become weak. Now they came killed, burned and looted."

Even as he spoke raw images of violence flickered across the screen. I stared as men, women and children scattered as invaders ran among them callously spearing everyone even the women and children. Some fleeing people climbed onto kiva rooftops then plunged down the entrance hole seeking any refuge that might come from the spirits of the ancestors.

Running Bear shrugged. "But the ancestors never came. It was as if the Anasazi were forsaken. The attackers set fire to many of the kivas, the spiritual centers, in the belief that the Chacoans would be unable to communicate with their spirits," said Running Bear. "When the existence of life is threatened humans assume violent means."

"Why on earth did they not have warriors — an army to defend themselves?"

"You mean a fighting class? It did not exist. Warriors were few and far between. The Chacoans were mainly farmers, hunters and merchants. That was their strength. They were people of the sun."

The old Indian sighed. "Most families fled into the hills and mesas and sought refuge in places around the great river that would become known as the Rio Grande. But some stayed on and attempted to rebuild but Chaco was doomed because the environment had changed. It took many years to die."

Suddenly, everything changed. The images of the Chaco under attack were gone, and so too was the desert. I caught my breath, we were now in the Great Cave and Running Bear was standing in front of me.

"Today, when you visit the pueblos for the most part they are the descendants of the survivors of Chaco," he said as if nothing had happened. "The pueblo people carried with them something they had learned in the last days of Chaco. It was called hurt anger and it took many years before these diseases left the descendants and the spirits of the ancestors returned in comfort."

"How did the tribes find the energy vortexes known as geospirals?" I asked.

"When a tribe was moving, the shaman would lead the way. He carried a prayer stick laced with beads, feathers and fur. They were also called talking sticks," said Running Bear and even as he spoke, one appeared in his hand. "Look."

He walked slowly across the floor of the great cave and as he moved closer to the geospiral I knew was there, the feathers fluttered and the beads clicked. As it became centered the prayer stick seemed to shake and vibrate. Running Bear glanced at me. "That is how the shamans found the voice of the earth, your geospirals. Then they knew where they would create their kiva and build a pueblo around it."

"A prayer stick is much like dowsing rods," I suggested.

"It's what you might call show business," remarked the Indian with a faint grin. "You can do exactly the same thing by holding out the palm of your hand and feeling the energy."

"Were you a shaman?"

He sniffed. "I still am. Shamans never die they simply change vibration," he said then quite upbruptly he held his hands together as if a Buddhist. "That is enough for today. Go an explore the energies in Santa Fe but first go to the land of the so-called Bandelier people. They left signs and messages."

"Can I...?" I started to say but the wind hissed and I found myself back in bed at the Sonterra condominium. A feeling of tiredness swept through me. Betty Lou was fast asleep and as I started to fall asleep I glanced at the clock...it was just after two a.m.

Suddenly I was wide awake. How was the time still the same? Was the excursion to the Chaco a lucid dream? Was it really an astral projection? Was time brought to a standstill? Shouldn't the interlude have taken some time, a few minutes at least? The whole thing was baffling. Some time later I drifted off to sleep.

9

GEOSPIRAL ENERGIES INSPIRE

Slender, like a willow branch, he was just eighteen when he first came to the Enchanted Land around New Mexico's capital Santa Fe. The high and rugged Pecos region of the Sangre de Cristo Mountains where the winds often frolic through the mountain passes carrying the aroma of pine needles appealed to his inner nature. He sat on his horse and took in the beauty of the raw country and sensed the energy with its invisible but powerful hands beckoning and pulling him to stay.

The year was 1922 and he had just graduated from the Ethical Culture School, an upscale Jewish High School in New York that prided itself on producing intellectuals. Plagued by an illness, the lanky, seemingly nervous teenager had been brought to the outdoors of New Mexico for the sole purpose of toughening him up

Horseback riding and hiking near the small and remote village of Cowles relaxed his mind, body and spirit and he was thrilled in 1928 when his family leased a large rustic cabin with a magnificent view of the Sangre de Cristos. They ultimately purchased it in the late 1940s.

The young man was J. Robert Oppenheimer and he would go down in history as the Father of the Atomic Bomb. During the 1930s he and his brother Frank ventured on long and often dangerous treks across the mountains and valleys sometimes without food, simply exploring the wild and spectacular country. On one of these trips Oppenheimer discovered the Los Alamos Ranch School at a place called Otowi.

It was a private and very remote boarding school for boys whose parents wanted their sons to receive a down to earth gentleman's education. Founded in 1917 by a Detroit businessman, Ashley Pond II, it comprised a community of rugged log cabins heated by log burning fire stoves, horses, harsh bitter winters made worse by driving winds and a generally rigorous, unforgiving outdoor life. An interesting phenomenon: the school was renowned for its healthy lifestyle and very few students ever quit. One wonders if Ashley Pond was aware of the powerful energies resonating at Los Alamos.

The school produced such controversial people as William S. Burroughs, the novelist who wrote *The Naked Lunch,* and Gore Vidal who brought homosexuality into the spotlight with *The City and the Pillar,* John Crosby and the American musician who went on to create the Santa Fe Opera was also educated at the school. Ashley Pond's daughter Peggy Pond Church born at Watrous a community on the east side of the Sangre de Cristo Range, became a renowned New Mexican poet and author.

It was violence happening thousands of miles away that started to seal the fate of the Los Alamos Boys School. It happened that day in December 1941 when the Japanese bombed Pearl Harbor and triggered a series of events that brought the war to the tiny mountain community in New Mexico.

It was in 1942 when Oppenheimer and Lieutenant General Leslie Groves set out to comb the south-west search for a site that would become America's first national laboratory. The physicist remembered the boys school and took the General to the community of Otowi. The trek gave Oppenheimer the ability to spend time in a place he had come to love in the Enchanted Land.

The two explorers needed a place that could be sealed off from the world, have a mailbox and administration office in Santa Fe and be allowed to fast track a theory called the atomic bomb. Otowi perched on the hill which ultimately became known as Los Alamos fitted the bill exactly. The rest is history.

Is it strange that many centuries before a tribe of the Keres Indians established several small communities in the region? We know that because they left a a vast legacy of petroglyphs — signs and messages from the past.

Back in the 1980s Betty Lilienthal and Dorothy Hoard became aware of the rock drawings throughout Los Alamos County and started mapping and studying them. Jim Lilienthal and Judy More did the photography. The book they produced and entitled *Sentinels on Stone* vividly shows the creations of the prehistoric Tewa ancestors.

They found a number of concentric circles – spirals — representing the Cosmos and one complete geospiral shown on page 11. The art forms in the rock carvings are quite precise. Three Kokopelli spirits are seen with their flutes serenading a well defined spiral next to them. If you have not encountered the name before Kokopelli is a fertility deity, usually depicted as a humpbacked flute player often with a huge phallus and feathers or protruding from the head

In the study the petroglyphs of humans are also well defined so one is left wondering about the people illustrated with box heads and box bodies. One such boxy character has one hand point to earth, the other pointing to the stars. There are several box-head petroglyphs in the collection but a design we found interesting is a face inside a circular capsule that has what the authors term a "panhandle" protruding. The picture begs the question: Is this a small space shuttle. It bears an uncanny resemblance to early NASA space capsules, the Gemini and Mercury types that landed in the oceans.

Today, the town is the home of the Los Alamos National Laboratory and over 18,000 people live in the County. When it comes to quality of life Los Alamos has frequently scored top marks on lists of America's Most Livable Places.

We wanted to take a dowsing view of the place. We quickly discovered what the ancients knew that the place has some very active geospirals. One wonders if J. Robert Oppenheimer felt the power too. The atomic bomb was created, tested and functioned all within the space of a scant three years. In anybody's language that is an accelerated accomplishment. There are some people who refuse to think the bomb was created in so short a time. There are others who know that when you work in the area of influence of a geospiral one can expect miracles or near-miracles.

We paid two visits to Los Alamos, one in 2010 to take photos and the other in 2011 to dowse the energies. We quickly found three in the center of town. One is in the block of 20th Street flanked by Central Avenue and Deacon. There is a clinic nearby which should benefit from positive energy given off by the spiral. We then walked through the park, passed the small lake named after Peggy Pond and tested the dowsing rods.

A second geospiral is in the parking lot of Los Alamos County Police Department flanking Oppenheimer Drive and Trinity Drive. In theory, the officers of the law should be a generally healthy lot coming under the influence of such earth energy. Again, one wonders why the Native ancestors ever left the area.

The third geospiral is to be found in the Fuller Lodge built in 1928 as the Ranch School dining room and kitchen. It also served as guest and nurse's quarters and contained quarters for staff. Named for Edward P. Fuller, a staff member at the Ranch School, it is made of 771 massive sawmill cut ponderosa pine logs, personally chosen by architect John Gaw Meem and Ranch School Director A. J. Connell. The building still stands today as an architectural tribute to the old school.

The energy emanating from the geospiral is positive and healthy and would inspire to extraordinary levels anyone living in the area. During the Manhattan Project it served as a dining room and kitchen. It is little wonder the complex is now a community building and is used for social gatherings and meetings. It houses the Art Center at Fuller Lodge, the Archives and Research Library of the Historical Museum, and the Los Alamos Arts Council. We have not to date had the opportunity of measuring the areas of influence of this trinity of geospirals but it could cover an area several hundred yards in radius, perhaps more.

It is good to understand that energy from geospirals can heal, inspire and balance one's energy. If one spends some time in the area of influence of a geospiral these qualities will quickly be realized. However, let us not confuse geospirals with doing good or bad. The Universe including Planet Earth does not judge us or the places it serves. Flowers do not judge each other. Can you imagine a rose saying to another rose "I am more beautiful than you." It is only humans that get invoved in the useless egotistical action of judging and comparing. Geospirals are neither good nor bad. They emit energy which heals and inspires. If one abuses it, then the force becomes negative. It is simply there like a mountain spring. Water contains benefits for all if it is used correctly. If used incorrectly it has the power to drown. Such is the power of the geospirals. They are exactly like mountain springs.

TASK FOR DOWSERS: Study the three geospirals mentioned above, determine their areas of influence. Check to see if there are more geospirals in Los Alamos County. Check to see where the leylines are located.

10

SANTA FE: HOT SPOT
FOR ENERGIES AND SPIES

After the first atomic bombs were detonated and further tests were conducted at a place clled Bikini Atoll in the Pacific the spies converged on Santa Fe which is a short 36 miles from Los Alamos. The city which is the capital of New Mexico served as an administration headquarters for the Los Alamos scientists and their families It was the Manhattan Project's shady and discreet window to the outside world. The room at the back of a Sena Plaza alcove between 107 and 109 East Palace Avenue served as a reception center for incoming new employees and all contact incoming and outgoing was carried out here. Project personnel received mail at P.O. Box 1663, Santa Fe, N.M., a facility at the old Santa Fe Post Office which is now the impressive Museum of Contemporary Native Arts, 108 Cathedral Place.

Project director J. Robert Oppenheimer and many of the top scientists spent much of their free time in Santa Fe and frequently haunted the bar of La Fonda, 100 East San Francisco Street but they were never out of sight of government security agents. Still, during the war many of the Santa Fe residents became aware that something important was taking place at Los Alamos simply because the population of the mountain village went from a mere handful of people to over 3,000 almost overnight.

Countless numbers of books, features and movies have been made on what happened after the bombing of Japan and how the old city of Santa Fe became a place for spies and counter spies. Some were discovered, others got caught.

The key players in this strange drama were Klaus Fuchs, a naturalized British citizen and one of the Project's top physicists who gave vitally secret information to Harry Gold, a courier for a Soviet spy ring. In Albuquerque Gold met David Greenglass an army sergeant who had been recruited into Soviet espionage by his wife, Ruth Greenglass, at the behest of his brother-in-law, Julius Rosenberg and wife Ethel.

When the whole scheme fell apart with arrests. Harry Gold and David Greenglass both served prison sentences. Julius and Ethel Rosenberg were executed in 1953 after being convicted of conspiracy to commit espionage during a time of war. The charges related to their passing information about the atomic bomb to the Soviet Union. This was the first execution of civilians for espionage in United States history. Klaus Fuchs confessed in Britain and was sentenced to 14 year imprisonment for treason. He served nine and later worked for the Institute for Nuclear Research near Dresden, East Germany where he received among other awards the Order of Karl Marx.

Thus, Santa Fe has become over the years a fascination for people who wish to stand on street corners, stare at buildings and feel the energies left by the scientists and spies of the 1950s.

But enough trivia, let us stay in Santa Fe, the capital city of New Mexico because it contains two powerful geospirals, both inherited from ancient Indian pueblos created by the Anasazi, the people from beyond the sun and a very old leyline.

LEYLINES AND ENERGY HOTSPOTS

Today, the energies manifested in Santa Fe are mixed but very real. The name of the city itself in Spanish means Holy Faith and in the European era it has existed as a community, a trading and communications center since 1607. It was designated a city in1824. Its full name is "La Villa Real de la Santa Fé de San Francisco de Asís" or "The Royal Town of the Holy Faith of St. Francis of Assisi."

Where Santa Fe stands today was once the home of a collection of Pueblo Indian villages from around 1050 to 1610. Tewa-speaking Indians possessed pueblos on the site and they knew and worked with the earth energy. Historians claim the sites of the pueblos were abandoned long before the Spanish arrived but Indian sources reject the claim.

The first Governor-General of New Mexico was Don Juan de Onate who in 1598 established the capital at San Juan Pueblo, 25 miles north of the present Santa Fe. After Onate retired, the new Governor-General Don Pedro de Peralta moved the capital to Santa Fe. The year was 1610. Incidentally this was a decade before The Pilgrims arrived at Plymouth, Massachusetts.

This makes Santa Fe the oldest U.S. city that is also a capital. At an elevation of 7,000 feet it is also the highest capital in the United States and is a growing city with a population of around 70,000.

We noticed an incredible number of healing and wellness facilities and one practitioner said: "In Santa Fe there are over 4,000 healers performing Reiki, massage, meditation, Yoga, spiritual and clinical counseling, intuitive arts, Buddhist retreats, Balinese spa treatments, facials, reflexology, hot stone and Thai massage, rose petal baths, acu-puncture, oriental medicine, osteopathic and chiropractic techniques, homeopathy, hypnosis and shamanic healing." How many artists call

131

Santa Fe home? Just about as many as healers we were told. You can find artists, writers, crafts people working in studios in just about anywhere there is a space. With such a resident population it is little wonder the city attracts tourists like bears to a honey pot.

A liberal community in a location of desert and mountains the people are very friendly and generally laid-back. Santa Fe is often called the 'Land of Entrapment' because most people who live there for a significant amount of time either never leave or return eventually full time. "Some believe this is because of the intense energy the town possesses," said a local resident on the Urban Dictionary website.

Back in the 1980s Oscar-winning actress Greer Garson who lived at nearby Pecos funded the creation of a state-of-the-art sound stage for the growing motion picture industry. The British-born actress from Manor Park, Essex donated millions for the creation of the Greer Garson Theater at the Santa Fe University of Art and Design. Incidentally until the end of 2011 the total number of films with Santa Fe area locations exceeded 350, some of the last being *True Grit, Cowboys and Aliens* and *Thor* says the Internet Movie Data Base, IMDb.

Georgia O'Keeffe frequented Santa Fe from her home in Abiquiui which is set among some of New Mexico's most spectacular and colorful rock formations.

In the 1920s and 1930s authors of many genres were resident or spent time in Santa Fe. There's a book devoted to this subject: *Santa Fe and Taos: The Writer's Era, 1916-1941* by Marta Weigle and Kyle Fiore.

Six blocks from the Santa Fe Plaza is a rambling adobe villa known today as the Inn of the Turquoise Bear, a bed and breakfast establishment. Formerly the home of Witter Bynner the American poet and scholar, for years it became known as the gathering and visiting spot for outstanding people. They included D.H. Lawrence — who spent his first night in an American home in this house, Willa Cather, Ansel Adams, Igor Stravinsky, Edna St. Vincent Millay, Robert Frost, W.H. Auden, Stephen Spender, Aldous Huxley, Clara Bow, Errol Flynn, Rita Hayworth, Lynn Riggs, Christopher Isherwood, Carl Van Vechten, Martha Graham, Robert Oppenheimer, Georgia O'Keeffe, Mary Austin, Willard Nash, Thornton Wilder, J.B. Priestly and many others. As Mabel Dodge Luhan's place in Taos was the gathering point for celebrities in Taos, so Witter Bynner's was the gathering place in Santa Fe.

Chances are it felt good to be there because it stands close to the areas of influence of two geospirals radiating healing and creative energies and several triple leylines.

THE SPIRAL MIRACLE

Remember the Los Alamos scientists gathering in a downtown Santa Fe hotel called La Fonda and being watched by spies and counter-spies? Well, just across the street there is a quaint little place called the Loretto Chapel. For the tourists who flock to it and the couples who launch their married lives in its ancient walls there are two obvious and very visible mysteries.

Inside the Gothic structure is a very special staircase often referred to as miraculous, inexplicable, marvelous and is sometimes called St. Joseph's Staircase. It is a phenomenon that confounds architects, engineers and master craftsmen.

The beautiful Gothic Loretto Chapel itself was designed by French architect, Antoine Mouly and his 18 year-old son Projectus brought in from Paris by Bishop Jean Baptiste Lamy who needed a classical European designed cathedral for the diocese.

While in Santa Fe Mouly was asked to design a dream chapel for the Catholic sisters who had arrived in 1852 and opened the Academy of Our Lady of Light. The Chapel was completed in 1878 and to the nuns consternation it was found there was no way to access the choir loft twenty-two feet above.

Frantically, the nuns called in carpenters to address the problem but they all concluded access to the loft would have to be by ladder as a staircase would interfere with the interior space of the small chapel. There was no way the nuns were going to climb ladders.

Legend says that to find a solution to the seating problem the Sisters of the Chapel made a novena to St. Joseph the patron saint of carpenters. On the ninth and final day of prayer a man with a donkey and a toolbox appeared at the Chapel and announced he was looking for work.

If you saw the excellent 1998 award-winning movie *The Staircase* starring Barbara Hershey, William Petersen and Diane Ladd you will know the legend of the stranger coming to the chapel and offering to build a staircase. The sisters accepted and over the weeks and months an elegant and very beautiful staircase appeared.

It makes over two complete 360-degree turns, stands 20 feet tall and has no center support. It rests solely on its base and against the choir loft. The risers are all of the same heighth, their number being 33, the years that Jesus lived on Earth. It was built with wood from trees long extinct. In addition it was constructed with only square wooden pegs without glue or nails. This phenomenon occurred between 1877 and 1881.

To add to the first mystery of how it was accomplished, there is another. The stranger simply disappeared one night without thanks or payment and was never seen again. The sisters searched for the carpenter and even advertised for him but in vain. There were strong suggestions that the stranger was a manifestation of St. Joseph the Carpenter. Who knows? While critics pooh-pooh the story, the fact is the miraculous staircase is there.

The Loretto Academy was closed in 1968 and the property was put up for sale. At the time of sale in 1971 Our Lady of Light Chapel was informally deconsecrated as a Catholic Chapel and is now a private museum operated and maintained in part for the preservation of the Miraculous Staircase and the Chapel itself.

The original staircase was built without railings and these were added as a safety measure. In addition because wedding couples are photographed on the staircase simple stabilizers were added to the staircase to prevent swaying.

There had to be a geospiral close by and sure enough there is. It radiates a globe of energy just in front of the Loretto Chapel altar and visitors who sit and rest or meditate for a few minutes will feel its rejuvenating energies and depart invigorated and feeling good. The area of influence extends across the chapel and out into the street.

In addition to the geospiral there are two leylines, one running a few feet parallel to the Chapel axis and the other outside. This other force is a triple hairline ley and it runs from outside the Chapel, through the La Fonda Hotel, through the Santa Fe Cathedral and along to a hill-top place known as Old Fort Marcy Park.

Fort Marcy was never a big time, active fort. It came into being during the American-Mexican war of 1846. It was a hexagonol structure with adobe walls nine feet tall and five feet thick. In spite of the fact it was designed to accommodate almost 300 soldiers, the troops and horses stationed there were billeted down in the town. The fort never acquired any real history until after it was abandoned in 1868

How it was finally demolished is another story. A lady visiting the territorial capital along with some friends in1887 discovered a large cache of Spanish coins hidden beneath the walls of the old fort. The lady claimed there were 2,300 coins dating back to 1740 and 1726. The Silver City Enterprise in reporting the discovery wrote: "After the discovery was made, large numbers of Santa Fe citizens turned out and dug the whole country up in the vicinity of the fort, but without finding anything new."

The frantic hunt for possible other hidden treashers doomed the old fort. The standing walls were reduced to rubble. The government sold the Fort Marcy location at auction in 1891. The city of Santa Fe acquired the site on the hill in 1961, landscaped the place and established a scenic overlook of the city.

Spirits tell me that the flat topped hill used for Fort Marcy overlooking Santa Fe was used by Native Indians hundreds of years before the coming of the Spanish.

Note for Dowsers: Check the Old Fort Marcy Park for a geospiral and check for additional leylines.

THE CATHEDRAL AT SANTA FE

Betty Lou and I visited Santa Fe for three days in 2010 and browsed all the tourist spots including the Loretto Chapel and the Cathedral and I was not keen on moving around with a couple of L-rods in the search position for all to see, particularly in religious institutions which warn that everyone is under video surveillance. In spite of the fact that Moses and several other biblical figures were dowsers, spiritual places particularly churches have attendants who frequently frown upon dowsers and politely reject an application to dowse such venues.

A veteran dowser would suggest deviceless dowsing. This quiet practice is by using the fingers to get a "yes" or "no" response. One rubs the thumb and forefinger together and asks the question such as "Is there a geospiral located in this room." In my case the rubbing feels rough for a negative (No) and smooth for a positive (Yes). Therefore dowsers resort to deviceless dowsing but only when the L-rods or pendulums are completely forbidden as in casinos and the stock markets.

I really had no intention of dowsing Archbishop Lamy's Cathedral Bassilica of Saint Francis of Assisi in Santa Fe. It just happened that my old buddy in spirit, my healing guide Chang kept on insisting: "You must spend the day in Santa Fe and find the geospiral there."

"Where?"

"In Archbishop Lamy's Cathedral," he replied.

When spirits are that insistent I know there is some deep reasoning at play.

As you move through the Cathedral's monstrously heavy doors laiden with religious pictographs, the first thing one sees are warning signs that the visitor is under video surveillance.

Being a deceptive dowser is not one of my best qualities but circumstances forced me to hide my dowsing tools. Two L-rods were slipped over my leather belt and dangling under my long jacket. Had there been anyone seemingly in authority I would have gladly asked permission but except for morning tourists and some people kneeling in prayer there was no one around.

The Cathedral is a beautiful place in all its aspects. It was designed in Romanesque Revival style with Corinthian columns and sweeping arches and is easy to photograph with existing lighting. Its European origin and designs are evident and the place is a credit to both the architect and the archbishop.

Suddenly, my spirit guide Chang urged me to look up at the images set in the upper walls just below the roof. One was a spiral.

"You see," he said.

I took several photographs. "Is that all?" I asked with a shrug.

"If you recall it is exactly the same spiral design the historians at Los Alamos found among the petroglyphs and recorded in their book Sentinels of Stone," remarked Chang. "It is the only one in the building."

We walked along the side aisle of the great place and discovered a leyline. If it was supposed to run down the axis it failed because it was set to the right. It disappeared into a wall.

"What's in there? Beyond the wall?"

"The Chapel of the Blessed Sacrament," said Betty Lou.

To get to the Chapel one has to walk to the far side of the Cathedral, pass through a door and turn to enter. We felt the energy the moment we entered. All the pews were empty and in spite of a note warning of surveillance cameras I pulled out the dowsing rods and went into the Search position.

"Is there a geospiral in this room?" I queried

One rod answered in the affirmative.

"Show me the center of the geospiral."

The rod swung and pointed along the aisle to a point by the altar. As I walked past it the rod turned and pointed in the opposite direction. We had crossed the center. Using two rods in search we found the center just in front of the altar. The Position was exactly the same as the old church at Arroyo Seco.

Again using the rods, I walked back down the aisle to the rearof the Chapel searching for the circular lines of the geospiral. The rods crossed at almost every other step. The geospiral energy lines were close and compact.

"There's a lot of energy in this place," I said to Chang.

"For people who come here either to pray or attend a service they are subjected to a very powerful healing energy," he said. "You can feel it, yes?"

I nodded an affirmation. "When Bishop Lamy and the French architect Antoine Mouly built this place they must have been fully aware of what they were doing. They must have felt the power of this geospiral. After all, it covers not only the chapel but also the front of the main church and the altar."

Chang smiled. "Lamy would have accepted it as the Hand of God."

"And the old pueblo ancestors, the Indians?"

"The Cathedral Park is situated at the center of the old pueblo and the geospiral is exactly where they had their kiva, their sacred space," he said. "It's a good place for receiving healing both physically and in the mind. It's best to sit and meditate for a while."

"I think I'm right in saying the Catholic Church stopped providing hands-on-healing some years back," I said to Chang. "But do you think they knew that if people wanted healing they could get it directly from the earth or the Hand of God?"

Chang shrugged. "Perhaps you are giving too much credit to the priests. This is a very good and powerful healing spiral but if you wish to see another and take some healing energy home you must go to Chimayó."

I agreed and recalled Dennis Wheatley had suggested that in his book *The Essential Dowsing Guide.* As we drove away I could not help but wonder how Dennis, tucked away in England could have known these things.

"He was a dowser," quipped Chang with a laugh.

11

THE HEALING HOLY DIRT AT CHIMAYÓ

There's something mystical and alluring about El Sanctuario de Chimayó. You can feel it as you park the car and join the throngs of pilgrims flocking to the site tucked away in the foothills of the Sangre de Cristo Mountains. It has been compared to Lourdes, the small market town lying in the foothills of the Pyrenees in France famous for the Marian apparitions of Our Lady of Lourdes that occurred in 1858 to Bernadette Soubirous.

Here at Chimayó the corridor is packed with crutches left behind by grateful people who have come, been healed and walked away. Testimonies that something different happens here.

The devotion of believers is far reaching. On Holy days such as Easter many pilgrims trek the roads to the Sanctuary, some as far away as Albuquerque ninety miles to the south. Some will attend the Catholic services, others determined and eager will push straight through to the small room adjacent to the church where one finds healing and something called the "Holy Dirt."

We had been to Chimayó twice before and in spite of years of training and working in metaphysics I had always carried a marked degree of skepticism. This, in spite of the fact I am a certified hypnoanalyst and fully conversant with the power of positive suggestion particularly in healing and in the treatment of psychosomatic illnesses. In a trance state induced by a hypnotherapist patients will often image chronic pain moving from one part of the body to the other and even "let go" of discomforts borne in the body for years. The fact that an old discomfort can be moved by the power of their own mind often assists in fast recovery. There again, I have had several clients once freed of their plight complain that they want it back. One even beat my chest in frustration because the pain had gone. Perhaps they see it as a cross to bear or some karmic debt. So, I seriously pondered how healing works at El Sanctuario as it is called.

My spirit guides suggested I return to Chimayó for a third time, take my dowsing rods and start my narration at the beginning.

El Santuario de Chimayó is a Roman Catholic church in Chimayó, New Mexico, USA. (Santuario is Spanish for "sanctuary".) Like the Cahokia mounds this shrine is a National Historic Landmark famous for the story of its founding and a contemporary pilgrimage site. So strong are its powers of healing its fame attracts over 300,000 visitors a year and this number is expected to grow. Often compared to Lourdes the Church claims it as the most important Catholic pilgrimage center in the United States. My question was will dowsing prove that healing energies prevail in this Sanctuary?

Chimayó is about 28 miles north of Santa Fe nestled in the foothills of the Sangre de Cristo mountains. It is situated in a fertile valley nourished by the waters of the Santa Cruz River. The village was founded in the late 1600s by Spanish settlers mostly experienced in farming, raising cattle, sheep and goats and weaving.

A seemingly idyllic life was always overshadowed by a fear of attack from marauding Indians, so to protect themselves they constructed the fortified plaza of San Buenaventura — now the Plaza del Cerro. It is said to be the last surviving fortified plaza in the United States.

The talents of those early settlers are still carried on by their descendants today including high-quality traditional weaving, growing red chile peppers, horse and sheep raising and cultivating large fruit orchards. The shops at Chimayó are famous for traditional Hispanic and Tewa Indian arts including wood carving, paintings of saints on retablos or flat wood slabs and bultos or sculptures, tin working and the ancient art of colcha embroidery and pottery. Colcha? Colchas are embroidered woolen textiles depicting religious images or scenes from everyday life.

Back in the early 1800s there were about nineteen families residing and working in the verdant pastures of the place called El Potero de Chimayó. The land where the Sanctuary now stands was the property of Don Bernardo Abeyta, one of the first members of Los Hermanos de la Fraternidad Piadosa de Nuestro Padre Jesús Nazareno otherwise known as Penitentes.

Like most sacred places there are legends. A popular one states Don Bernardo became deathly ill and one night a spirit or angel came and took him to a location where the earth possessed special healing powers. He took some of the dirt in his hands and was immediately cured. Don Bernardo was so overcome with relief and joy he built a small chapel on the spot. The year was 1813. Word of Don Bernardo's healing spread rapidly and sick people started to flock to the chapel at Chimayó but the original chapel was so small it was decided to replace it with the present church. That was 1816.

There is another fascinating legend surrounding the old place. A friar while performing penances observed a strange light streaming from a hillside near the Santa Cruz River. The curious friar began digging and discovered that the source of the light was a crucifix. The object was taken and placed in a nearby church. Next morning it had disappeared and was found mysteriously placed on the hillside. This happened three times. At that point it was decided to build a chapel. The year was 1813.

Whatever its origin, the Sanctuary remained in the family until 1929 when the owners faced financial difficulties and were forced to sell. Purchased by the Spanish Colonial Arts Society it was later donated to the Archdiocese of Santa Fe.

The Sanctuary on Juan Medina Drive in Chimayó and is easily recognized by a framed picturesque adobe arch which is part of a walled courtyard. The old chapel is built of adobe and is 60 feet long and 24 feet wide. The walls are a hefty three feet thick and two bell towers crown the entrance to the building. The elegant doors were carved by the 19th-century carpenter Pedro Domínguez.

Once inside the chapel there is little to differentiate it from many other chapels in villages scattered around New Mexico. It is dark and somber with an altar wall appearing like a huge ikon surrounding the image of Jesus crucified. Some of the visitors to Chimayó attend mass and services but most visitors are drawn to the rooms adjacent to the chapel and most have to stoop to enter. Coincidentally, it is similar to the Church of the Nativity in Bethlehem, one has to duck to enter.

The room to the right is relatively bare and adds to the mystique. It's like stepping into a medieval prison cell with a bare floor except a small round hole about 18 inches across that captures the visitor's eyes. It is filled with dusty brown earth and is not very attractive. It is called el pocito or the little well. A sign declares the earth is "Holy Dirt" or "Tierra Bendita."

If one sits and silently observes one can witness something resembling healing happening. Some people simply kneel, pray and let their fingers wander through and caress the earth. I watched a tiny lady dressed in black get down on her hands and knees beside el pocito. A younger woman, perhaps a helpful teenager helped the woman get down onto her knees. One could sense her pain. Her old hands carefully fondled the earth while her lips moved in silent prayer. She knelt there in silence for perhaps 30 seconds, then suddenly without any help, climbed to her feet, nodded to her stunned teenage helper, bowed to el pocito and made the sign of the cross and walked out totally unaided. Healed? I have no idea, but one thing is for sure, in a short space of time the old lady had changed. A faint triumphant smile flickered on her delicate white face as she pushed her way out.

Some people purchase little plastic cups from the Chapel's bookshop at $3.00 a piece. They show the name and a picture of Sanctuario de Chimayó imprinted on the lid.

Many of the visitors describe the healings as miracles because it's a good word and one really does not have to understand the phenomenon anyway. But there is little doubt that the Holy Dirt carries with it some healing power although the Catholic Church, aloof and judgmental as usual, takes no position on whether miracles have happened or not. However the Archdiocese is beginning to cash in on Chimayó as we shall see.

Many visitors carefully fill the little plastic cups with the "Holy Dirt" and take them home often in hopes of a miraculous cure for themselves or someone who could not make the trip. Some pilgrims taste or even eat some of the dirt. Most pilgrims seeking healing rub themselves with the Holy Dirt or simply keep the cups among their spiritual souvenirs are home. An adjacent Prayer Room displays many ex-votos as well as photographs, numerous discarded crutches which line the walls and other comments on those said to be healed.

Incidentally, ex-voto is a Spanish word meaning votive offering. It hails from the Latin meaning from a promise or vow. They are there for all to see, some very personal yet all expressing faith in God and thanks for favors received. When you stop to read them one cannot help but feel the deep emotions of love being expressed and shared.

As I waited outside el pocito another lady who once upon a time must have been tall and erect entered the room. She propped a walking cane against the wall and knelt down by the hole. Her gnarled hands seemingly suffering from arthritis, gripped the edge of the hole, then slowly as if something had had given her permission she allowed her fingers to feel the dirt. Lips moved in in a silent prayer. Then as if what she expected was accomplished, she climbed to her feet, gazed back down brieflyat the little well and walked through to the chapel.

"Hello, you've forgotten your cane?" I called out.

Surprised, she slipped back into the room, seized the cane and walked past me, flashing a nice smile. "I don't think I will need this for now," she said and left it among the crutches. I watched her leave the chapel. She stood taller than when she had entered.

The little stone well containing the Holy Dirt does not have an endless supply. Several times a day chapel staff replenish the dirt in el pocito with earth obtained from the pastures a short distance away. Total dirt supplied this way totals a mind-boggling 25 to 30 tons a year. At Easter when over 100,000 visitors turn up chapel attendants refill el pocito every hour.

When cynics and skeptics hear this they often sneer "So much for Holy Dirt. That's holy crap." Luckily, not all think this way.

In the world of dowsing, earth energies and particularly geospirals there is an answer and the knowledge is quite revealing.

DOWSING THE POWER OF HOLY DIRT

We stood on the street overlooking the chapel grounds. It was late afternoon in October and the tourists had dwindled to just a few. I walked slowly along the street with my dowsing rods in the search position. They crossed quickly three times in close succession indicating the existence of a leyline with three parallel hairlines just as British dowser Dennis Wheatley suggested in his book The Essential Dowsing Guide.

The triple hairline comes from across the street and runs parallel by about 18 inches to the right of the main axis of the Sanctuary. Beyond the church the leyline continued through some trees and a new chapel development and then continued across the pasture beyond into the hills.

Once we established the leyline in the chapel, I asked one rod if there was a geospiral in the area. It responded in the affirmative and pointed in the direction of the adjoining rooms. Like most religious places the management does not generally approve of people wandering around with either cameras or dowsing rods so Betty Lou stood in the chapel talking with the sister while I surveyed the adjoining rooms where el pocito is located. Betty Lou did reveal to the sister that I was a dowser tracking earth energies but I think the sister really did not want to see me do it.

Although I endeavor to dowse with rods without anyone watching a young couple from Oregon spotted me: "Wow! You're dowsing," said the man quickly. "You can sure feel the energy in this place. You must be getting some good readings."

"Do you dowse?" I asked.

"No," came the reply, "but my Dad did in the Marines and he learned in Vietnam looking for Vietcong tunnels and hideouts. He served on a special dowsing unit."

So I went searching for a geospiral. I lowered my head and walked into the adjacent prayer room containing photographs of healings, countless discarded crutches, and other testimonials of those purportedly healed. This was not el pocito or the little well room. I moved to the far end of the testimonial room by the door leading outside.

"Show me the geospiral center," I asked the rod. Suddenly it twisted around and pointed towards el pocito.

"Show me the energy rings."

Holding the double rods I immediately picked up one energy ring, then another and another. The rings were intense and quite close together. I kept walking into the little room the home of el pocito. In spite of the tight conditions the rods showed me the rings of a powerful geospiral and the center was El Pocito – the little well.

Chang came to my side realizing a question was burning in my mind.

"This is a sacred healing point," he said softly. "It radiates healing energy continuously. It comes from the Spirit of the Earth."

"Yes, I can feel the energy exactly as I did at Cahokia and Santa Fe and the other places," I replied. "It's very strong and positive."

Then I raised the question uppermost in my mind. "But how does it make the Holy Dirt a healing power? The dirt comes from the fields, the old pastures. The Sanctuary staff admit it in brochures and publicity. It is no secret."

"Impregnation," said Chang easily. "When the Sanctuary staff refill the little well the earth energy of the geospiral immediately bathes the dirt with its curative powers. It happens all within a few minutes — actually no time at all. It is very powerful."

"So based on what you are telling me when people stand here and pray they are being healed and when others fill the little round plastic caps with dirt and carry them home they are taking the healing power with them," I suggested.

"Two years ago when you made a brief visit to el Sanctuario you filled a plastic capsule, took it back to your home, placed it in your office with the cap on. Listen, it works better with the cap off," said Chang quietly. "When you return home use your pendulum to check the power of the Holy Dirt."

I did. The pendulum and a single dowsing rod recorded circles of energy flowing round the capsule. Hairlines of energy alternated in circles round the capsule fanned out the important healing force. If one starts six feet away the bands of energy are several inches apart and as the rods or pendulum close in the bands are about an inch apart.

Chang's revelation was stunning.

"So this is why miracles occur," I responded knowing exactly what Chang would say next.

"There's no such things as miracles only physical events which Earth people fail to understand," responded. "But it's all right if they like to think of them as miracles."

"Thinking back to the times of the ancient Greeks they had healing temples," I said. "Were they endowed with healing geospirals?"

Chang nodded vigorously. "They were and still are," he declared. "But most people ignore them because they have lost touch or fail to understand." He paused for a few moments. "You may wish to put the question of healing to Running Bear next time you meet."

Energy is a strange commodity. I recall being at the Spiritualist Church at Westville, New Jersey and a well known lady from the church was in hospital. Someone had a soft blue cushion. Each member of the congregation held the cushion for a few moments, blessed it and impregnated it with loving thoughts and healing energy. The cushion was taken to the hospital and the sick lady gratefully kept it on her bed and within a few days made a remarkable recovery. It is a great technique for anyone to use. The energy from the geospiral at el pocito works the same way.

ANOTHER SURPRISE AT CHEMAYÓ

Outside the main chapel at Chemayó we walked into another surprise. It happened this way. The whole place had changed in a year. The owners, presumably the Catholic Church – the Archdiocese of Santa Fe — have built an outdoor amphitheater as part of a chapel complete with altar and rings of permanent stone seating behind the original Sanctuary. As we watched, workmen were still completing the landscaping.

The sister explained it was being built because too many people wished to attend the regular services and the old chapel was not big enough to accommodate them, thus the need for a new chapel nearby..

Moving to the rear of the Sanctuary outside my dowsing rods again picked up the three hairlines of the leyline coming through the church. It was interesting to note that the triple leyline passes through an ancient cottonwood tree and then runs through the altar of the new amphitheater-chapel and disappears into the foothills of the Sangre de Cristo Mountains. Whoever planned the new amphitheater-chapel knew exactly where to place the altar because it not only coincides with the triple hairline leyline it borders another geospiral.

Walking with the dowsing rods in the search position, I started from the outer limits of the amphitheater moving towards the altar. Coincidentally as I passed each row of seats the rods crossed indicating an energy line from the geospiral. Incredibly the circular rows of seats match the rings of the geospirals so that whoever sits in a seat at the new amphitheater will be open to receiving healing energy from the Earth.

One wonders if the church management knew these sacred earth energies existed and did someone who possessed the intuitive talents of the ancients pick that spot for the new altar? Or were the planners and architects guided by spirit? Guessing I would say someone is going to say it was an Act of God. That just about covers everything.

I find that when one asks a question and gets an answer in metaphysics two or more questions crop up. It becomes quite frustrating at times.

Now here's another intriguing point we observed at Chimayó. In the yard or gardens at the back of the church where the new amphitheater chapel has been built, there exist several old and gnarled cottonwood trees. All of them are mostly bare of religious ornaments except one. On the chunky bark of one tree that has no designation at all hundreds of people have pinned or attached crucifixes and other religious ornaments, some with names and some without. There are also makeshift crucifixes, little twigs neatly tied together and pinned or stuck to the tree. In addition there are also crosses in tin, metal and ornate silver. One crucifx was lovingly made of tightly rolled aluminum tinfoil. As we stood there gazing at the tree one could not help but feel love and prayers of the pilgrims that had passed this way.

Now here's the clincher: It is the only tree that stands on the triple leyline that runs through the El Sanctuario de Chimayó. Did anyone ever tell these pilgrims about earth energy? I doubt it, but somehow a whole lot of people mysteriously felt the healing power calling to them and started to adorn the old tree with crosses.

The fact that El Sanctuario de Chimayó possesses a triple leyline and two strong geospirals is reason enough for pilgrims from far and wide to converge on the place every year. It is little wonder that many call it the Lourdes of North America.

The Sanctuary of Chimayó is a National Historic Landmark and wouldn't you know that research shows it was once the site of an Indian Pueblo as the population started to leave the ancient Chaco Canyon. The Pueblo Indians built numerous settlements along the Santa Cruz river and its tributaries and at least 33 prehistoric sites have been documented, one of them at Chimayó.

As we search for the big geospiral, perhaps a vortex, we realize we are following in the footsteps of the Native Ancestors.

So now we must go to the Taos Pueblo.

TASKS FOR DOWSERS: Study the Chimayó leyline, follow its directions both ways and check its origin. If the terrain becomes difficult resort to map dowsing.

12

A THOUSAND YEARS AT TAOS PUEBLO

The Taos Pubelo is one of the most northern Native Indian communities still very active and moving into the 21st century. Three miles north of the City of Taos it is picturesque in that it sits at the base of New Mexico's highest mountains. Its adobe multi-storied homes capture the focus of thousands of tourists every year. Artists and photographers such as the great Ansel Adams have set up their tripods to catch this glimpse into history. The Taoseans will tell you it has been in existence for a thousand years so they were probably the first of the Tewa-speaking Chaco citizens to read the writing on the doomed Canyon wall and migrate into the welcoming valley of the Rio Grande.

Archeologists and the Indians themselves say the main parts of the present buildings were constructed between 1000 and 1400 A.D. Little has changed in the buildings since the first Spanish explorers arrived in northern New Mexico in 1540 and believed that the Pueblo was one of the fabled golden cities of Cibola. The two oldest structures are Hlauuma (north house) and Hlaukwima (south house) and are considered to be the oldest continuously inhabited communities in the United States.

Some 150 Taoseans live in the Pueblo year round and another 1,800 live on the Taos Pueblo lands. Most do not use electricity or indoor plumbing choosing to maintain the old traditional modes of life. If you need Native

Indian drums or moccasins, Taos Pubelo is the place to find them. They are very skilled at leather work. If one pauses to view the scenery on the way in or out you will see the spacious puebloean pastures that are home to a herd of 200 buffalo plus cattle and horses.

A healthy stream named Red Willow Creek or Rio Pueblo de Taos winds its way through the Pueblo. The merchants in their little adobe shops around the plaza will tell you it comes from the mountains, specifically the Blue Lake, a place they revere and hold sacred.

If explorer Coronado and his Spanish army failed to find gold today's descendants of the Chaco Natives have found theirs. One, they operate the Taos Mountain Casino and two, there is a seemingly never-ending stream of national and international tourists relentlessly heading for the Pueblo to curiously explore the adobe buildings, enjoy native foods and browse through the quaint little shops.

Of course, there is an entry fee and if you carry a camera, there is a fee for each one you carry. There are "off limits" signs in the private areas of the community and visitors are warned not to climb any ladders leaning against buildings. The Taos Pueblo is open daily except when closed occasionally for ceremonial purposes. Some spiritual ceremonies are open to the public but cameras and recording devices are not allowed at these events although in this day and age it must be difficult for Taos Security to watch for disguised recorders and cameras buried in cell phones.

The largest event of the year is the San Gerónimo Feast Day on September 30th. If you're visiting, it's always a good idea to tune into their website at Taospueblo.com.

THE MYSTICAL SIDE OF TAOS PUEBLO

The inhabitants of the Taos Pueblo are for the most part Catholics and like most Catholics they cling defiantly to the dogmas and ways of the church although many Indians one encounters either within the Pueblo or outside insist in the mysticism of the old ways.

Carl Gustav Jung the Swiss psychiatrist who possessed an unflagging interest in philosophy, Spiritualism and metaphysics led many to view him as a mystic although his true ambition was to be seen as a man of science, a researcher and enquirer into the higher life.

It was in the winter of 1924-1925 that Jung spent several months in Taos observing the lives of Mabel Dodge Luhan and her clan but also attempting to fathom the mystical side of the Native Indians.

Jung interviewed the Chief of the Taos Pueblo Ochway Biano who proclaimed rather bluntly that all whites were mad. When Jung questioned this he was told that whites think with their heads and not with their hearts.

Immediately, the Swiss psychiatrist went into a long meditation and for the first time in his life, or so it seemed to him, someone has created a picture of the real white man.

In his book *Memories, Dreams, Reflections* he says the Pueblo Indians are unusually closed mouthed and when it comes to religion they are absolutely inaccessible. It was because of this block that Jung said he abandoned as hopeless any attempt at direct questioning.

He openly expressed surprise because he had never faced such an atmosphere of secrecy. He noted that today all the religions of civilized nations are accessible and sacraments have long ago ceased to be mysteries.

Jung expressed astonishment when he realized the emotions of Native Indians change when they speak of religious ideas. In routine day-to-day life the Indian shows a degree of self-control and dignity but when he speaks of the tribal mysteries he is in the grip of a surprising emotion that he cannot conceal. This became evident when I had a conversation with a Taos Pueblo businessman as we shall see.

As Jung continued his interview with the Chief, the Indian although frequently evasive to questions, tears would frequently come to his eyes. They were seated on the roof of a Taos Pueblo building. The Chief pointed to the sun and asked "Is not he who moves there our father? How can anyone say differently? How can there be another god? Nothing can be without the sun." He then added: "What would a man do alone in the mountains? He cannot even build his fire without him."

Jung went on to ask the Chief if he thought the sun might be a "fiery ball shaped by an invisible god." He found his question aroused neither astonishment nor anger. Ochway Biano replied: "The sun is God. Everyone can see that."

Another day, Jung and the Chief were standing by the river when an elderly Indian, vibrant with suppressed emotion came up and asked the visitor: "Do you not think that all life comes from the mountain?" It was a far-reaching question and Jung acknowledged that the mountain is evident of this fact. He wrote: "Obviously all life came from the mountain, for where there is water there is life. Nothing could be more obvious."

Carl Gustav must have left wondering what the Native Indian's idea of a mystical religion actually entails.

We visited the Taos Pueblo twice to search for an energy source in the shape of a geospiral. The lady at the ticket desk charged us for entrance and two cameras. Striving to be totally honest I explained to the two office clerks that I was a dowser and seeking earth energies. I showed her the two L-rods.

"Oh, I don't know if that is permissible," commented the first one. She turned to check with the other woman who shrugged as if my activities were of no importance.

"Don't do it in front of the visitors," said the first woman.

"Thank you for your understanding," I said with a smile.

The church overlooking the Plaza is the Church of San Geronimo or St. Jerome. Catholic and quite imposing, it was built in 1850 to replace the old church which had stood since 1619. Enclosed in a thick white adobe wall with an arched entrance and a cross at its apex from inside one can view the entire Plaza and all the buildings around.

I stood by the walls and used one rod in the search mode. "Are there any geospirals within the Pueblo?"

Two, came the reply.

"Show me the first one," I asked expecting the rod to point into the church. It swung round and pointed the other way to the tall cedar pole standing alone in the center of the plaza.

Using both L-rods in the search position I started to walk towards the giant pole, focusing on geospiral energy. The rods responded quickly and strongly showing each of the spirals rings until I reached the great pole. Pocketing the rods, I placed my hands on the bare wood and a flood of earth energy came up into my body like a swirling torrent. It was resoundingly positive and healing. An aura of elation and clarity swept around me.

This ceremonial pole is the center of life in the Taos Pueblo. Like Jung and many other researchers besides myself, I pondered on the existence of another side, a more mystical side other than the commercial side of tourists buying drums and jewelry and leather products, photographing the ancient adobe multi-level homes and wandering around munching on Native Indian pastries.

I recalled reading a blog written by Marti Fenton otherwise known as White Deer Song. It was the medicine name given to her by her husband Blue Spruce Standing Deer.

Marti's writing gives us an insight into the higher mystical nature preserved by the Native Indians. It happened at the colorful Turtle Dance at the Pueblo.

"One New Year's morning we went to the Turtle Dance at the pueblo. After religiously attending every public dance at the Pueblo for many years I hadn't been to a turtle dance since Standing Deer's mother passed five years ago. Now I'm stepping back into that once familiar environment again feeling a bit like I'd returned from exile.

"It transports one to another reality beyond time, as if nothing at all had happened in the past 1,000 years," she says. *"The adobe buildings of the village rise organically from the clay earthen skin of Mother Earth, completely unaffected by the town of Taos and 2012 just two miles away.*

"The Pueblo blends like old furniture in the great room of Taos Mountain secure in its forever place against the sharp blue sky. The smell of wood smoke brings memories from ten years ago and lifetimes ago. This is life transcending the accustomed sectioning into years and culture," she noted and added that even with the mixture of native and town people dressed in both contemporary and traditional styles, it has no effect on the overriding ambiance.

The ceremony, she wrote, *"cloaks everyone within range in timelessness. As soon as you step onto the reddish gold dust of the plaza, the spirit of the pueblo ancestors overtakes whatever you came with. The dimension-*

al door opens and the Old Ones pour out onto the plaza mingling with their descendants and surrounding everyone in their medicine."

The dancers who embody their spirit, she adds, are bare chested except for their red body paint even though the temperature is below freezing. Their feet rhythmically, reverently tap the mother's body. Gourd shakers send cascading shivers through our bodies. These songs awaken something absolutely primal and timeless even in visitors. This is why we are here," said Marti.

According to native lore, the turtle carries all of our troubles on her back and that is why she moves so slowly. *"What does speed and time have to do with the real world? As I feel my body, vibrating subtly from the inside out with the rhythm of the dancers and the deep hum of their song I wonder if this isn't a stronger more elemental world than the one existing just a few minutes down the road. How can we now believe there is only one world and it is the real one?"*

Delving into deep philosophy she poises the question: *"Could it be that this ancient world of golden tan clay and brilliant sky like the turtle carries our confused world on its back and subtly, simply transports us to the fundamental world, the one beneath all the other worlds, the original home of us all?"*

Today the Taos Pueblo stands as a beacon of the old ways shining a light of awareness into a world. We must remember it was the force, the earth energy that drew these Tewa-speaking people to this place centuries ago, and it still holds them here. But the price has been heavy.

The dowsing rod in the Search position showed there were two geo-spirals. One is in the central plaza so where was the other one? The rod went through a series of pointings and I followed it. First to some little shops, then to a cemetery and then the ruins of an old adobe church, its bell tower still intact but the old walls were mostly crumbled and in ruins. This was the original Church of San Geronimo built in 1619.

Running Bear's voice came from behind. "Now you are getting into the rough stuff."

TAOS PUBELO – A HOTBED OF REVOLT

Someone once told me "If you need fighting Indians look to Taos Pueblo. They breed them there." But that was difficult to marry that statement to the Native Indians I encountered there." Apart from a sign at the entrance to the Pueblo which declared "Office of the War Chief," there was nothing to suggest fighting. Sonny Spruce, a merchant who sold me a fine Native Indian drum told me the War Chief guards the Pueblo land against uninvited intruders. I trust I was not intruding.

In the beginning the lands that are now known as New Mexico were ruled by Spain and the Europeans brought new ways of living particularly in farming. In addition they brought so-called protection from Apache and Navajo raiding parties, new rules imposed by a new administration, a new religion, and they carried all the European diseases particularly the devastating smallpox along with syphilis and whooping cough.

The protection was sparse and therefore insufficient and the Roman Catholic religion was no match for the mysticism and spirituality of the old religions and the Indians quickly turned back to the ways of their ancestors.

For over a decade around 1660 the Spanish administration banned the spiritual Kachina dances by the Pueblo Indians and ordered the Franciscan missionaries to seize every mask, prayer stick, and effigy and ceremonially burn them. Spanish officials who understood and sympathized with the Indians and attempted to curb the power of the missionaries were charged with heresy and tried before the dreaded Inquisition.

The smoldering restlessness within the pueblos was about to fester and burst. One incident that triggered the revolt occurred in 1675 when the Spanish Governor Juan Francisco Trevino picked up intelligence of an upcoming meeting of the tribal medicine men. Troops invaded the meeting and forty-seven were arrested. Three were executed and the others were released with warnings not to continue meetings and sedition must stop.

Enter Popé, a Tewa Indian Chief and a celebrated medicine-man from the pueblo of San Juan also known today as Ohkay Owingeh or Place of the Strong People. The Pueblo is about 25 miles north of Santa Fe. Popé (pronounced Po'Pay) was a survivor of the Spanish execution but upon returning to the San Juan pueblo he realized he was under close surveillance by the Spanish authorities. One night he silently slipped away and headed for the Taos Pubelo where he knew the people were ardent supporters of his plans.

Popé revealed to the Taoseans that while he was in a kiva powerful spirits had come to him and inspired him with their thoughts and energies.

The command was clear: the Spanish must go! Spanish rule must be eradicated. The attack would be totally coordinated and simultaneous. Thousands of Native Indians from different tribes across thousands of square miles would take part. The Taos Pueblo became a hot bed of intrigue.

The target time was a specific date in August 1680. Having no calendars a system of knotted cords was created as a means of keeping track of the days. Runners carried them to the various participating tribes. The instructions were, one knot was to be untied for the passing of each day and when no knots were left — that was the day for the uprising.

Unfortunately, two days before the special day two messengers were captured and under torture revealed the plot. When the Indians realized their plan had been uncovered the message went out: "Attack immediately!"

The revolution erupted on August 10th 1680 and the heated uprising quickly turned bloody. Led by Taos, Picuris, and Tewa Indians in their respective pueblos twenty-one of the territory's 40 Franciscans were slain and another 380 Spaniards including men, women, and children were slaughtered.

Spanish survivors fled to the safety of Santa Fe but the Indians raced after them and laid siege to the fortified city and the Governor's Palace. After two days of siege the Indian force dammed the small creek and promptly cut off water supplies. During August in Santa Fe water supplies are critical plus there were food shortages. Governor Antonio de Otermin ordered a retreat and Spanish troops managed to get the survivors out of Santa Fe. The Indians watched from the hills as the convoy headed south out of New Mexico.

The Pueblo Indians endeavored to wipe out all traces of the Spaniards and Christianity but this proved difficult because the Europeans had brought changes that had been embedded in Pueblo life, notably iron tools, horses, sheep, cattle and various vegetable crops and fruit trees.

The Spanish were gone from New Mexico for twelve years. Eventually they returned with a new attitude and a different administration which issued land grants to the Indian Pueblos. They renewed promises of protection from raiders from the north but it was an uneasy truce with occasional flare ups. The new administration always maintained a close eye on Taos Pueblo mainly for the role Taoseans played in the 1680 ousting.

We shuttle forward to events involving two geospirals, one at the old Church of San Geronimo and the other on Mount Lucero, the place I call Lawrence's Cave.

The year is now 1847 and blood will flow again right on the dusty lanes of Taos Pueblo.

TAOS PUBELO UNDER ATTACK

The U.S.–Mexican War was an armed conflict between the United States and Mexico from 1846 to 1848. It occurred in the wake of the United States annexing Texas which Mexico held as a territory along with California and New Mexico. In the American takeover, the army invaded parts of northern New Mexico Territory. They advanced on Santa Fe and installed Charles Bent as U.S. Territorial Governor. Bent was a frontier's man, a mountain man and a fur trader and in 1835 he married Maria Ignacia Jaramilla who was born in Taos. Maria's younger sister Josefa Jaramillo would later marry Kit Carson. Bent was appointed Governor of the Territory of New Mexico in September 1846. As it happened he lived a short term in office.

Somewhere along the way a resistance movement to United States control was established by the Taos Pueblo Indians but it was badly organized. Then on a cold windy morning on Tuesday, January 19, 1847 the Pubelo insurrectionists launched the revolt in Taos that would be forever remembered in American history.

Heading the rebels were Pablo Montoya, a Mexican, and Tomás Romero, a Taos Pueblo Indian. Little did they know they were initiating a costly and devastating blood bath.

Romero led a force of Indians and Mexican-Spanish settlers to the house of Governor Charles Bent in Taos where they broke down the door and promptly shot Bent with arrows They then proceeded to scalp him allegedly in front of his family. Thinking the Governor was dead they moved on. However Bent was still alive and with his wife Maria Ignacia and children plus her sister, now the wife of Kit Carson and Thomas Boggs the group escaped by digging through the adobe walls of the house.

Spotted by insurrectionists there was no escape. Bent was promptly assassinated but the women and children were left unharmed. The angry Indians continued their rampage and killed various other people and officials employed by the U.S Territorial Government.

The 700 insurrectionists were now fugitives and they fled helter-skelter to the Taos Pubelo with the U.S. Army in hot pursuit. Elders suggested the old Church of San Geronimo built in 1619 would be safe behind the thick adobe walls Besides no one, not even the Army attack a church. That idea was wishful thinking. Another point: The Army was fresh from the Mexican war and the Indians had not reckoned on the artillery the Army had brought with them — several small cannon and a new howitzer.

A GLIMPSE OF A BATTLE

"I would like to photograph the old church," I said to the lady at the Pueblo office.

"That's not possible," she replied. "It's off limits."

"It's to test the energy," I said truthfully. "Is there anything wrong with that?"

"It's a sacred place," came the reply. "You'd have to ask the War Chief?"

His office door was near by. "Could I speak with him?"

"He's away right now."

Finally she spoke to a companion and after a minute turned back to me. "That man there will escort you," she said, pointing to a well present-ed Pueblo staff member. A pleasant fellow, he listened intently as I explained that I wished to walk round the ruins of church and the grave-yard packed with crosses and grave markers of all shapes and sizes.

Feeling a little restricted and under guard we set off. It was a fairly warm October day and I was wondering where my spirit friends were when a young couple appeared seemingly out of nowhere and started putting questions to my escort. Naturally he had to stop and talk because that was his job Smiling, I walked on and walked the adobe wall perimeter by myself which was my original idea.

A Native Indian woman leaned out of a doorway: "You're off limits. Go back!"

"They said I could come," I called out.

The woman called back something but I failed to hear above the growing crescendo of noise. Noise? What noise?

The church behind the old adobe walls was resounding with a battle. Guns. Heavy guns. People screaming. Horses hoofs against stones. The crunch of heavy wheels. More screams. Somehow my intuitive abilities, my psychic ears were picking up an invasion, a battle.

It's called psychometry a metaphysical faculty I taught and practiced over the years. In essence all energy has a memory. Cosmically they are called the Akashic Records. Every atom, every molecule, every energy field is inter-relating with all energy fields adjoining hem and leaving records. For instance every person by their very thoughts and emotions leaves a record on their environment. If the dominant thoughts in a house are negative that house will hold those negative records for years even centuries after the family has gone. And vice versa, if the dominant thoughts are positive the records in that house will always feel positive and new people coming years after will feel those records..

As an example I once sat down by the Venetian walls of Nicosia on the Mediterranean Island of Cyprus and the energy in the old stones replayed the bloody Turkish invasion of the city in 1570. It was a vivid and somewhat shocking experience. I describe it fully on starting on page 47 in my book *The Quest of the Radical Spiritualist*. Anyone who develops their psychic senses can pick up images of events occurring many years ago. Psychometry is the 101 of learning to be psychic and because it covers space and time, I call it the Time Machine. It is an excellent learning opportunity for students and researchers.

But here and now I was listening to a battle that was recorded in the ruins of the church of San Geronimo at the Taos Pubelo 146 years before and I was not even touching the crumbling adobe walls.

"Ah, so, you are a time listener," said a soft voice beside me.

Immediately I recognized Running Bear.

"It's called psychometry or a measure of the soul," I said. "I like to think of it as a time machine. Yes, I suppose time listener is a good name."

"There was a massacre here," said the old Indian. "The puebloeans do not talk about it outside but they still remember it." I could feel his presence closing in. "Tonight when you are asleep it will all come to you in a dream."

"Like you told me about Chaco?"

Running Bear was a man of few words and had gone. The sounds of the battle were still with me as I continued to walk along the old walls stopping once to photograph the old bell tower standing defiantly in the intense bright sunshine.

At the far side of the cemetery I took a photograph of the crowded cemetery and the remains of the old church. One dowsing rod confirmed the existence of a geospiral in the church. Strong and radiating energy, the old church had been a sacred place for the Taos Indians. Incidentally, among the graves in this historic plot is the last resting place of Mabel's husband Tony Luhan.

My search for the vortex was begining to appear like a tapestry. Perhaps all the geospirals collectively were producing a vortex. Of course there could be others hidden away that could be found not necessarily on the pueblos or ruins of pueblos, but simply tucked away in the rocky landscape of New Mexico. The search for the geospirals was intriguing but I sensed there had to be a vortex somewhere to have attracted so many people here over the centuries.

As we returned to the Sonterra condominiums in Taos I wondered what Running Bear's dream would show me.

DEATH COMES TO THE PUEBLO

Spirits have no idea of time at least they always give that impression. I lay in bed waiting for Running Bear to come and must have drifted off to sleep because suddenly I was awake. The clock showed 2.07 a.m. Something inside me commented that two plus seven equals nine – the mystical number of the Cosmos. Feeling slightly disappointed I turned on my side and as I drifted off to sleep it happened.

A rush of wind, energy seemingly moving in all directions and then I knew I was flying, but where? A blink! I could see the church of San Jeronimo. It was now intact, a somber building standing bravely but dark in the swirling snow. People were running and sliding through the snow, calling out in muffled tones as if they did not wish to be heard. A large group of people huddled together outside the church. Their strained, anxious faces peered through the soft but swirling snow dancing like spirits in the breeze over the road from Taos.

It was past dawn and there was enough light for the Indians to make out a row of dark figures positioned across a field about 300 yards from the church. Figures on horseback stood silently watching as several horses pulling carriages containing field guns several small cannons and one new howitzer moved into positions.

"That's the American Army," said Running Bear in my ear. "They are extremely angry over the killing of the Governor and his people. The soldiers are seeking revenge. The killing should never have happened. It was wrong in the first place."

People started moving in and out of the church in the belief that its three-foot thick walls and the Creator would provide protection. An officer, perhaps a captain, accompanied by two juniors, all on horseback galloped to the outskirts of the pueblo like they had done for two days before.

As before he started to call out for the Indians to surrender.

A shot crackled out. The trio raced back to their lines. One man was wounded because when the trio stopped a figure fell from his horse. All was quiet. An ominous silence enveloped the road to the Taos Pueblo. This was the third day and the officers and men were becoming impatient. The cannons that had been used before were simply not effective against the thick adobe walls of the church. The two pound cannon balls simply ate away at the church edges or left little holes in the walls which started to appear like a pepperpot. Colonel Sterling Price gave the order for heavier artillery.

Suddenly a thunderous explosion rent the silence! A cloud of smoke bulged around a mountain howitzer perched on a horse drawn carriage. A shell hissed eerily through the cold air then crashed into the wall of a nearby adobe home which was blown to pieces. The explosion was ear-piercing. The howitzer spat again. This time the shell crashed into the higher wall of the church sending timbers and thatch coverings flying. Moments later flames and thick smoke started appearing over the church roof. The howitzer spat again. Another shell smashed into the church wall followed by a thunderous explosion. Part of the church collapsed amid clouds of swirling dust.

Suddenly there was no one to be seen in the pueblo and the infantry advanced. They reached the door of the church which was now locked and barred. An officer called for the surrender of the people inside, but hearing no reply, he ordered his men to withdraw.

The Army withdrew and returned a short while later. On the sixth call, hearing no reply he immediately shouted orders and soldiers armed with axes, sledgehammers and wooden posts started hacking at the adobe walls. It seemed futile, so they withdrew to allow the howitzer to fire two more shells. One was a direct hit and one of the walls fell open and the thatched roof started to burn furiously in several places and columns of dark grey smoke curled away towards the mountains.

As the U.S. Army started to return many of the Native Indians broke free from the church and started running into the wooded foothills hoping for refuge in the mountains. Some Indians stayed to fight the incoming troops. Hand to hand fighting ensued. Shots were fired. The smell of gunpowder and burning timbers filled the whole area. The ground quickly became littered with bodies and the snow turned red with blood.

Suddenly I felt Running Bear tugging my arm and the next moment we were over the treetops watching fleeing Indians running through the trees and along forest trails, pursued by American cavalry. We spotted several groups of Indians surrendering and being marched down the hill.

Then we were in the big cave the one I call Lawrence's Cave. Several Indians carrying wounded brothers had reached the sanctity of the huge cave. A small log fire was burning to provide light and everyone moving about left enormous shadows on the roof of the cave. Someone carrying a leather skin bag brought in water from the stream outside and another brought in leaves which were laid on the wounds. Several women arrived with deer skin bandages and these were applied to the wounded. Voices were soft and almost muffled as if by making sounds they would attract the army.

A young woman carrying salves and knives emerged from the growing darkness outside and gave them to a tall man. Suddenly she spotted someone she knew among the wounded and she rushed to his side. No cry of alarm. She placed her palms on his head and the pained expression on the young man's face seeped away. A few inches away an elderly man, presumably a medicine man, worked on the chest wounds of a thin, gawky looking man. Using a bone needle he carefully sewed up a laceration with a strip of tendon while beyond him a young Indian kneeling beside an older man, maintained a tourniquet on his leg just below the knee to prevent bleeding.

Then I noticed something.

The dozen or so injured men who had been treated were laid in circles around the small center stone, the place I had determined earlier as a geospiral. While helpers comforted and provided sustenance for the wounded they all knew of the healing power of the geospiral.

"The spirits from the Earth, the ancestors, are working to heal the wounded," said Running Bear. "You felt them before when you came with your rods."

"That was energy," I said quickly.

"Spirits are energy. I am energy and so are you, my friend. Surely you know that everything is energy." I could see the smile on his face as we floated above the scene.

"So this is how the old Church of San Geronimo was destroyed," I said.

Running Bear nodded. "Over 150 of our people died in that massacre. Six leaders of the insurrection were tried and hanged. History will show that it served no useful purpose. Violence rarely does."

"Something I cannot understand," I said. "The Anasazi at Chaco Canyon were peaceful people, farmers and hunters. I never heard of warriors there. What caused the Indians to rebel with violence against the Spanish and then the U.S. Army."

"Any man will fight for a cause he believes in. If the Europeans when they first came had respected the rights and the beliefs of our people this would have been a different land," said Running Bear. "But the descendants of Chaco learned new strategies after the massacre of 1847. You can witness that in the battle they carried out for the return of their land and Blue Lake."

The geospirals returned to my mind. "My rods said there are four. We found one in the old church, one at the ceremonial pole at the center of the Plaza, and there is one here at Lawrence's cave. Where is the fourth?"

"There is a kiva which is kept hidden from the tourists. It is considered sacred."

"It's not on any map of the pueblo."

Running Bear nodded. "It is on the maps. They call it the room in the earth or the underground chamber. It's where the spirits of the ancestors come and talk. It is necessary to maintain a good — how do you say? – energy.""

"That makes sense. Outsiders can unwittingly bring in negative energy."

Running Bear nodded in agreement. "However there is a fifth one and it is responsible for much of the health and wellbeing for many miles around the valley," he said quietly. It accounts for the longevity of many people in the region.

"And where is that?"

"The fifth one is at a place your people call Blue Lake."

"It's off limits."

"Go and read the story of the battle the people of the Taos Pueblo had with the fathers in Washington and then I will talk to you about the powers of the place the Indians call Ba Whyea.

When I woke up at the Sonterra condo I felt grubby and headed for a shower. I couldn't help feeling as if I had been in a smoky old cavern that reeked of blood and pain.

13

THE BATTLE FOR BA WHYEA

To all intents and purposes Blue Lake is the life of the Taos Pueblo. It sustains the agriculture and the livestock and the day to day living of the inhabitants. But Blue Lake is also the soul of the Taos Pueblo and the Indian people put up a prolonged and active but non-violent fight to get it back.

The problem started in 1906 when Blue Lake and the surrounding lands were taken – some say stolen — from the Taos Indians by the United States Government. It was to become part of the planned Carson National Forest established in July1908. Named after the American pioneer and Taos resident Kit Carson today it covers 1.5 million acres of forest lands in northern New Mexico.

Initially the Indians did not protest the takeover because they believed the sacred lake and the forest would be protected but the administrators, the U.S. Forest Service implemented a "mixed use" policy allowing for recreation, grazing, and resource extraction.

Bulldozers and earth graders moved in to make roads for loggers, hunters and campers. Prayer sticks and other spiritual markers were stolen or destroyed thus the idea of a protected region in and around Blue Lake evaporated.

Over the years the Taos Indians were offered cash settlements but these were quickly rejected. Meanwhile, new comers settled on the land and the community of Taos originally called Don Fernando de Taos was created on what were originally tribal lands. The community was incorporated as a town in 1934 with Mabel Dodge Luhan in the center.

In the 1960s the Taos Indians began a vigorous and far reaching publicity and media campaign for full title to Blue Lake and the surrounding lands. Newspapers and radio stations across the country backed the Indians claims. The Indian Claims Commission stated that the Taos Indians had been unjustly deprived of their properties. A monetary offer was forthcoming but the Taos Pueblo rejected it on the basis that their "Religion and Life was not for sale."

The National Council of Churches backed the Indians' claims but the U.S. Forest Service offered barren land the Indians did not want. Four bills were introduced in Congress and the Taos Indians and their supporters fought each one.

Blue Lake became known as a special and sacred place where the trees on the surrounding mountains were called "living saints." It was a special place not only for the Taos Indians but also the plants and the animals living in the region. The Blue Lake area provided plants used in medicine and rituals. It was reported that Taos Indians make two-day pilgrimages to the place they know as Ba Whyea to say prayers to the spirits and express a deep appreciation of all living things.

The media blitz intensified continually stoked by announcements and activities of the Taos Indians. Finally in December 1970 the Senate voted to return the Blue Lake and the surrounding lands to the Taos Pueblo. Thirteen days later on December 15th 1970 President Nixon signed the bill into law and the 48,000 acres of land that had been taken away 65 years earlier was returned. A great battle with no violence was over and now jubilation reigned.

In August the following year there were the official celebrations with prayers, songs, dances and speeches and a buffalo feast and all the Taos Indians wore their traditional and colorful ceremonial outfits. The return of the land was a tribute to the tenacity of the Pueblo leaders and it was fought without violence and bloodshed.

We wanted to see the Blue Lake, not simply because of the dowsing but because of the mysticism surrounding it and the heavy but invigorating energy that emanates from the mountain area. But I was to be disappointed.

We quickly discovered that the Blue Lake and the surrounding mountains and lands are off-limits to everyone but registered members of the Taos Pueblo. The Pueblo lands are extensive now totaling 99,000 acres. The village itself is 7,200 feet above sea level and Blue Lake is at 12,185 feet.

I checked in with Running Bear but immediately felt a block.

"You have the ability to project your higher mind and your astral body," he said easily. "Go if you must but I cannot assist you."

"It would be great if I had a horse and some cooperation from your people," I argued. "But the people at Taos Pueblo office state that to visit the Blue Lake one must be a registered tribal member and I am not,"

"Work with your mind," came the reply. "It's much faster than by horse." He spoke almost as if amused by the conversation.

"It's not the same. I love water. It would be good for me to feel it."

There was a distinct feeling that Running Bear was no longer listening. That's the trouble with spirit communication. They just break off when you least expect it.

THE MYSTERY OF BLUE LAKE OR BA WHYEA

One night I awoke at 2:00 a.m. and sensed an absence of spirits. Betty Lou was sleeping and the Sonterra condo felt very quiet. My desire to see the Blue Lake was burning in me. Running Bear's refusal to take me was understandable. In spite of being in Spirit for many centuries he still felt a distinct loyalty to his people and the desire of the Taos Indians not to have white people running around their sacred lands.

"You could always try astral travel," suggested Chang quietly.

A good idea but the truth is I am not a skilful astral projectionist. Way back in another time I studied the useful writings of Robert Monroe in *Journeys Out of the Body* and successfully flew across the Atlantic and visited my sister in England without any problems. Another time I broke into the Spirit World and saw some fascinating spirit-light demonstrations, got caught and was rebuked by an indignant ascended master. My healing guide Chang got me off the hook. Another time Chang took me to see my father working in a spirit laboratory. But apart from some relatively unconscious night excursions out of my body I had made no deliberate attempt at astral projection.

Systematically relaxing my body in bed, I allowed my physical form to feel heavy and let go of any tensions. Shortly after I started to feel light and sensed I had progressed through alpha into a theta state of consciousness. This is a level of consciousness where the body is asleep and the mind enters a dream state. Normally meditation is great for prompting lucid dreams where one is conscious that he or she is dreaming.

For a while I tried some traditional exercises for slipping out of the physical but nothing seemed to work. I waited for the rushing winds but they failed to occur.

Damn!

Perhaps I needed to go deeper so while working on this I tripped out and went to sleep. When I awoke it was getting light outside. Regretfully astral journeys would have to wait until another night so I sadly closed my eyes and started to slip off back to sleep. And that's when the rushing winds started.

As soon as I heard them I knew I had to focus on Blue Lake. For a few moments Ba Whyea became a mantra and I felt myself being pulled up out of my physical body, out through the roof and hurtling across town towards the mountains. I kept chanting. For a few seconds I had a fear of colliding with treetops. Taos Pueblo resting quietly in the grey light of dawn zipped by as did Taos Mountain. I could see a stream below, several waterfalls, a zigzag road that came to an end and a few seconds later a vision seem to be there in the haze. I paused hoping this was the way. Then it came zooming at me. From photographs I recognized the famous Blue Lake or Ba Whyea

But it was not blue. It just did not match the spectacle described by Indians and local storekeepers in Taos. It was dark and touched with the greys of dawn The fir trees had lost the early October snow of a week ago and a few patches of white adorned the pine covered ground. Some wildlife people told me that black bears and a few mountain lions patrol here along with elk, deer and bighorn sheep but there was little to see in the dawn light. I thought it was a tree stump and then it moved and materialized into the outline of an elk.

My feet touched the ground. It was soft and grassy. Some flowers from the summer now lay flat and lifeless. I wondered where the birds were because there were none to be seen and then I recalled we were at the 12,000 feet mark, a height above the bird line. The Sangre de Cristo

Mountains are known for the maximum height that trees will grow The tree line is in excess of 12,000 feet.

Walking down a small sandy slope I came to the water's edge and watched as my hand attempted to touch the water. It was difficult to feel but then I realized I was in my astral body which really has no physical feelings, at least that is what the so-called experts said.

The water was crystal clear but suddenly I could feel its energy, warm and invigorating. Suddenly I felt very awake and had to stay focused or I would be whipped back to my body. The powerful energy seemed to come up from the earth and move through my body. I wondered how I could feel its presence in my astral body.

"It takes practice," said a voice behind me. It was Running Bear.

Somehow his presence and his ability to read thoughts did not surprise me.

"You came on your own," he went on.

I nodded with a grin. "You don't have to be responsible for me."

"That is true," he said and with his hand he waved across the lake. "What do you see?"

"The lake and the mountains and the trees and the coming sun."

"Nothing else?"

Suddenly I realized he was seeing something that I failed to see."

"Look again."

The lake started to boil? No, that was not it. I could see the waves of energy rising like a mist, some from the water itself, some from the land and the rocks. It was as if the whole panorama was giving forth energy.

"How......?" I started to ask.

"You need to change your eyes and the way you see things. You would know it as your vibrations. Use your magic...your psychic sight...like you would see auras."

I did. Waves of multi-colored light shimmered as they rose up from not only the rocky beach but also the water. It seemed as if the water was alive.

"What is this? Volcanic mist?"

"No, it's the phenomenon for which you search," he said quietly. "As you call them – geospirals."

"Good Lord!" I gasped. "I have never seen a geospiral. I've always measured it with my dowsing rods and pendulums." As I spoke I felt as if I were a small boy again and listening in awe to a school teacher."How many?"

"Seven!"

"Don't they conflict with one another? They are so close and so intense."

"They work and communicate with each other."

"How?"

"All energies communicate with other energies. It's like humans communicating with each other." He paused for a moment. "I see in your history you visited Stonehenge in the country of your birth. Did you know that the stones talk to each other."

"That's impossible!" I responded. "They do not have a consciousness." I said it quickly and then realized I had made a mistake.

Running Bear grinned at my plight. "When you touch the stones as a time listener – performing your psychometry – you read the history of the rocks and you feel their heaviness, yes?"

I nodded.

"Everything has a consciousness. Not the way the intellectuals know it, but a consciousness, nevertheless," said the old Indian. "Even the sun and the moon possess consciousness as does the Earth. They are very important in our lives."

The idea left me pensive for a while.

"So there are seven geospirals here at Blue Lake. No wonder the Taos Pueblo people wanted this place returned. It is understandable," I said and gazed upwards. The energies were spraying outwards in the dawn like a huge mushroom filling the sky. That's really not a good description. The energy was expanding like a dome, similar to the dome we had experienced at Woodhenge in Cahokia, Illinois.

"It's like a vortex," I noted. "The earth is giving off continual flows of energies. Are they all positive. It's like a continuous bloom."

"They are, as you say, balanced," announced Running Bear then he drew closer. "Now you understand why the people of the Taos Pueblo come here for prayers, sacred ceremonies and some even come here before they die."

The last few words triggered the question. "Why?"

"To make peace with the gods of the Earth and express thanks for being able to live a good life on the planet," he said then added slowly: "At least some do. Those who believe in the old ways. Many of our people struggle with the Church on the one hand and the old ways on the other. The old ways are spiritual, the Church...?"

There were movements in the mist, the energy. Someone or something was moving through the energy. My hand pointed to the figure materializing.

"The ancestors are coming. They bathe in the energy. It revitalizes them and brings back memories of the years they were on Earth." Even as he spoke several more spirits materialized.

"Do they come up from the earth or do they come down?" For once I felt lost.

"They materialize. They change vibration. The Spirit World is all around you and all a spirit has to do is consciously change vibration to walk the earth. The vortex, your geospirals make it easy. For us it is like bathing under a waterfall. Beautiful and very clean. They wander through the trees and talk to the spirits of the forest."

Running Bear gazed at me with those dark brown eyes that seemed to penetrate into my soul. "You will write of your visit to Ba Whyea?" It was a statement more than a question.

"Will it worry you if I do?"

"No," he shrugged nonchanantly.

"That's good," I said. Then I paused and looked at him quizzically.

The old Indian shrugged again. "It matters not whether you do write or you don't write. Who is going to believe you? The lessons, my friend, were for you, a believer."

He shrugged and stared off into the rising sun. It was time to get back and even as I thought I was back in my body not asleep but wide awake.

Betty Lou woke up. I told her I would make tea after taking a shower, so I left the bed, walked across the carpet to the bathroom and the moment I trod on the tiles I felt particles of sand under my feet.

I froze! "That's impossible! My physical body never left the bed."

In the distance I could hear Running Bear chuckling.

"Spirits!" I muttered and headed for the shower.

THE ENCHANTED LAND

It was little wonder that the entire region flanked by the mysterious Sangre de Cristo Mountains on the east and the valley of the Rio Grande is referred to as the Enchanted Land. The highway encircling Taos, Questa, Red River, Eagle Nest, Angelfire back to Taos is named the Enchanted Circle. It goes round the very center of a vortex, a powerful set of geospirals much the same as the energies at Sedona. Glastonbury, Stonehenge, Mount Ararat and Everest.

The area of influence of the Blue Lake vortex easily embraces the town of Taos and it is little wonder that it attracted the energies of men and women who rode the waves of greatness and did not quite understand why they came. Those people have been mentioned in this book and there are many more artists, writers, musicians, poets, photographers who came and stayed for perhaps a few weeks, a winter, or even stayed for life. D.H. Lawrence eagerly looked forward to getting back but his body gave out and dashed his dreams. Georgia O'Keeffe with her paints and brushes roamed the area for over half a century until her eyesight failed her. Mabel Dodge Luhan, the celebrated society hostess and author equaled O'Keeffe's time here as did Lawrence's typist Lady Dorothy Brett who became a great south-western artist in her own right.

The people at the Taos Pueblo may or may not be aware of the powers and the gifts of the Blue Lake or Ba Whyea — but how long will the old ways protect and keep it isolated. My memory banks recall visiting Sedona in Arizona some twenty years ago when the population was a couple of thousand and tourists hurtled by with only a few stopping to see the Bell Rock and bask in the energies of the Mesa Verde. Today, the resident population is over 10,000 but the annual number of visitors is over the 400,000 mark. They come to feel the vortex and bathe in the spiritual aura of the place.

Taos is expanding in a similar parallel. Even as I write this (April 2012) the influential Forbes magazine has declared that Taos has earned a reputation as one of the country's "most captivating small towns." Also the Smithsonian Magazine has just listed Taos as Number Two on its list of the 20 Best Small Towns in America. Captivating! That's a good word. Mabel Dodge Luhan would totally agree.

Somewhere in the Santa Fe region there is another vortex, of this I am sure, but where? I do not know. There are powerful geospirals in the downtown area, notably the Loretto Chapel and the St. Francis Cathedral Chapel and again at Los Alamos and again at Chimayó. The Native Indians, the descendants of Chaco Canyon knew of the powers of earth energies, the geospirals and built their spiritual centers on them and enjoyed healthy lives until the Europeans came with their heavy religious influences that failed to recognize and appreciate the earth energies.

Perhaps some dedicated dowsers will take on the task of mapping geospirals in the Enchanted Land. A good starting point would be to check all the places where pueblos existed and move on from there. Remember when the Europeans arrived there was an estimated 150 Indian pueblos in and around the Rio Grande valley in northern New Mexico. Dowsers should check existing old maps then using the rods in the search position check the location of old pueblo sites not listed. Then check for geospirals and leylines.

Dowsers have this ability and published reports will add to the history of the Enchanted Land.

14

EPILOGUE:
ARE GEOSPIRALS EVERYWHERE?

Somewhere in the middle of our treks through the Enchanted Land, Betty Lou raised an interesting supposition. "Suppose for instance," she said, "these geospirals are created by human beings gathered together for prayers for healing, energy and to give thanks to God. Could this mean that we humans, using the power of prayer and thought can create a geospiral in any given place?"

"This raises the question," she added, "does the earth respond to such prayers and focuses healing energy through the geospiral systems?"

We decided that while the questions deserved some consideration there were indeed some further thoughts. How many geospirals does it take to make a vortex? We determined there were seven at the Blue Lake. Can one consider a geospiral on its own as a small or mini-vortex?

Expert dowsers like the late Dennis Wheatley in the United Kingdom suggested that most geospirals are indicative of blind springs, underground domes of pressurized water. While we ascertained that most of the geospirals found in northern New Mexico are very close to running streams, only one was over a blind spring and that was in the chapel at the Sanctuary of Chimayó which is close to a river. Blue Lake is a phenomenon in that it has geospirals in the water and on the land.

In all cases we found the presence of leylines, particularly triple haired leylines at all the places we checked physically.

SO ARE GEOPSIRALS EVERYWHERE?

Good question and it appears that geospirals are everywhere. When we returned to our winter home in New Jersey we decided to conduct a brief survey of obvious places in the nearby town of Mount Holly. The area was once occupied by Lenape Indians who sold their land to the first white settler Walter Reeves in the mid-17th century.

Now, the major difference between New Mexico Indians and tribes on the east coast is that the easterners have not left maps or many physical markers and indicators as to where they held their camps or spiritual services. Whereas in New Mexico the remaining tribal pueblos are still very active and those that were deserted have left kivas well entrenched in the ground at such places as Pecos, Bandelier and Chaco. One can guess at possible locations or use the dowsing rods to point to places where physical indictators or ruins are absent.

In Mount Holly there is a church once used by Catholics on Washington Street. Its use was discontinued some years ago when a new church, the Sacred Heart was built on the corner of High Street and Bartram Avenue.

We first dowsed the old church for geospirals and leylines but to our surprise found nothing. Moving over to the present church we found a triple-haired leyline running close to the axis of the building, but no geospiral.

At this point I used one rod in the search position and asked for the location of the nearest geospiral. It pointed to the adjoining Sacred Heart Parish House and in particular a small chapel that flanks the building.

The building according to Barber and Howe in their Historical Collections of the State of New Jersey 1844 show that in the village there are "several elegant dwellings, among which is conspicuous Dunn's Chinese cottage, erected by the proprietor of the late Chinese Museum in Philadelphia. It is at the base of the mount, at the western entrance of the town, and is a combination of the Chinese and English cottage style. The grounds are tastefully arranged, and the general effect of the whole is light, fanciful, and extremely picturesque."

Somewhere in its history the house became the home of a cloister of nuns and part was converted into a chapel. The nuns have long gone but the chapel is now known as the Chapel of the Blessed Sacrament. Yes, it contains a strong geospiral.

Its center is just in front of the altar similar to the one in the Chapel of the Blessed Sacrament in the Cathedral at Santa Fe. This geospiral has close systematic rings and covers much of the building but the area of influence does not reach the body of the church. Here again if one sits in the chapel for fifteen to thirty minutes there is a distinct superior feeling of rejuvenation and healing which is typical of the phenomena.

In the search for geospirals close to the Chapel the rod suddenly swung round and pointed across the street to the mount, a forested area covering two to three city-blocks and flanked by the Mount Holly Cemetery. It is mentioned in the Barber and Howe description above and is the mound that gave Mount Holly its name in 1931 following a referendum. It has an abundance of holly trees.

We entered through Hillside Avenue and climbed the rough pathway to the top of the mount. There are two National Geodetic Survey markers and the one at the very top also marks a geospiral with an area of influence of about 25 yards. The day we climbed The Mount was windy, dowsing was difficult and we were forced to end the visit. We did however sense the presence of Native Indian ancestors — spirits.

TASKS FOR NEW JERSEY DOWSERS: map the location of Indian communities in the Mount Holly region and check for more geospirals.

TASKS FOR DOWSERS GENERALLY

Search your immediate areas for leylines and geospirals. Make maps.

Check residences that are in the Areas of Influence of geospirals and question people as to the condition of their health.

Check churches, historical sites, hospitals and health centers for geospirals and leylines.

Always check geospirals for blind springs and nearby rivers, creeks.

If possible hold a meditation or prayer service around a geospiral. Say a prayer of protection and be prepared to communicate with any spirits that may be attracted.

In your searches know that if you have discovered a group of geospirals – five, seven or nine – that you have a vortex. Measure its Area of Influence and check to see how it impacts the region and in what ways.

Finally, always ask questions and take photographs and keep records of all phenomena encountered. You will be glad you did.

For Betty Lou and I our plans are to continue our search for geospirals and vortex wherever the rods, our intuitions and the helpers in Spirit take us, perhaps new horizons, perhaps back to the Enchanted Land for more studies of Holy Dirt and Sacred Earth.

THE END

SOURCES THAT MAY HELP YOU

BOOKS ON DOWSING & ENERGY

The Essential Dowsing Guide by Dennis Wheatley / Celestial Songs Press

Avebury: Sun, Moon and Earth By Maria Wheatley, Busty Taylor / Wessex Books

Discoveries of a Master Dowser by Maria Wheatley / American Dowser Digest Fall/Winter 2010

The Pattern of the Past by Guy Underwood / Abelard-Schuman Ltd.

Crop Circles by Lucy Pringle / The Pitkin Guide of Jarrold-Publishing

The Ley Hunter's Companion by Devereux & Thomson / Thames and Hudson

Earth Magic by Francis Hitching / Picador – Pan Books

Pendulum Power by Greg Neilsen / Destiny Books

Journeys Out of the Body by Robert A. Monroe

INSIGHTS: The Healing Paths by Robert Egby / 3 Mile Point Publishing

BOOKS ON NEW MEXICO

Anasazi America by David E. Stuart / University of New Mexico

Los Alamos & the Pajarito Plateau by Snyder, Gibson / Los Alamos Historical Society

The Magic of Bandelier by David E. Stuart / Ancient City Press

The Earth Has A Soul: C.J. Jung by Meredith Sabini / North Atlantic Books

Sentinels on Stone by Betty Lilienthal & Dorothy Hoard / Los Alamos Historical Society

A Coming of Wizards by Michael E. Reynolds / Solar Survival Press

Mabel Dodge Luhan: New Woman, New Worlds by Lois Palken Rudnick / University of N.M.

Edge of the Taos Desert by Mabel Dodge Luhan / University of N.M.

Winter in Taos by Mabel Dodge Luhan / Las Palomas de Taos

Lorenzo in Taos by Mabel Dodge Luhan / Sunstone Press

The Delight Makers – a novel by Adolf F. Bandelier / Harcourt Brace Jovanovich Inc

Utopian Vistas by Lois Palken Rudnick / University of N.M.

The Taos Indians by Blanche C. Grant / Rio Grande Press

Santa Fe & Taos by Marta Weigle & Kyle Fiore / Ancient City Press

The Legendary Artists of Taos by Mary Carroll Nelson / Watson-Guptill

The Spell of New Mexico Edited by Tony Hillerman

Frommer's New Mexico - 9th Edition by Lesley S King

Top Ten Santa Fe, Taos & Albuquerque / DK Eyewitness Travel

Of Time and Change by Frank Waters / MacMurray and Beck

The Man Who Killed The Deer a novel by Frank Waters / Washington Square Press

Inventing Los Alamos by Jon Hunter / University of Oklahoma Press

The Woman Who Rode Away by D.H. Lawrence / Penguin Classics

The Serpent's Tongue (Prose, Poetry & Art of NM Pueblos) Edited by Nancy Wood / Dutton Books

Taos Pueblo and its Sacred Blue Lake by Marcia Keegan / Clear Light Publishers

Ancient Peoples of the American Southwest by Stephen Plog / Thames and Hudson

A Taos Mosaic, Portrait of a New Mexico Village by Claire Morrill / University of N.M.

DVDs / FILMS

The Mystery of Chaco Canyon, narrator Robert Redford / Bullfrog Films.

Bandelier National Monument, Sky Island narrator Meryl Streep, Western National Parks

The Atomic City with Gene Barry / Oliver Films

INTERNET

The Ancient Spiral Encyclopedia – www.ancientspiral.com

The Taos Pueblo - www.taospueblo.com/

Artists in Taos - www.taospainters.com

Earthship Biotecture – Taos - http://earthship.com/

Los Alamos & Atomic Energy Foundation - www.mphpa.org/classic/index.htm

OTHER BOOKS BY ROBERT EGBY

Non-fiction

Cracking the Glass Darkly: The Ancient Path to Lasting Happiness

The Quest of the Radical Spiritualist: The Journey Begins

INSIGHTS: The Healing Path of the Radical Spiritualist

KINGS, KILLERS AND KINKS IN THE COSMOS:

Treading Softly With Angels Among Minefields
(autobiography)

Historical fiction

PENTADAKTYLOS:
Love, Promises and Patriotism in the Last Days of Colonial Cyprus

THE GUARDIANS OF STAVKA
The Deadly Hunt for Romanov Gold

All books are available through good bookstores throughout the world.

CPSIA information can be obtained at www.ICGtesting.com
Printed in the USA
BVOW041035250213

314028BV00003B/6/P